DEMOGRAPHIC DEVELOPMENTS
AND ECONOMIC GROWTH IN NORWAY
1740-1940

DEMOGRAPHIC DEVELOPMENTS
AND ECONOMIC GROWTH IN NORWAY
1740-1940

Thorvald Moe

ARNO PRESS

A New York Times Company

New York / 1977

Editorial Supervision: ANDREA HICKS

———————•———————

First publication 1977 by Arno Press, Inc.

Copyright © 1977 by Thorvald Moe

DISSERTATIONS IN EUROPEAN ECONOMIC HISTORY
ISBN for complete set: 0-405-10773-0
See last pages of this volume for titles.

Manufactured in the united States of America

Publisher's Note: This book has been
reproduced from the best available copy.

———————•———————

Library of Congress Cataloging in Publication Data

Moe, Thorvald.
    Demographic developments and economic growth in
Norway, 1740-1940 : an economic study.

    (Dissertations in European economic history)
    Originally presented as the author's thesis,
Stanford, 1970.
    Bibliography: p.
    1. Norway—Population. 2. Norway—Economic
condition. 3. Norway—Emigration and immigration.
4. United States—Emigration and immigration. I. Title
II. Series.
HB3615.M58 1977   301.32'9'481   77-77190
ISBN 0-405-10802-8

DEMOGRAPHIC DEVELOPMENTS AND

ECONOMIC GROWTH IN NORWAY 1740-1940:

AN ECONOMETRIC STUDY

A DISSERTATION

SUBMITTED TO THE DEPARTMENT OF ECONOMICS

AND THE COMMITTEE OF THE GRADUATE DIVISION

OF STANFORD UNIVERSITY

IN PARTIAL FULFILLMENT OF THE REQUIREMENTS

FOR THE DEGREE OF

DOCTOR OF PHILOSOPHY

By

Thorvald Moe

May 1970

ACKNOWLEDGMENTS

Most of the research work on which this dissertation is based was carried out in 1968 and 1969 while I was a graduate student in the Department of Economics at Stanford University. I am deeply indebted to Professor Moses Abramovitz who, as a teacher, scholar, and advisor exemplar, gave me his continued support and aid throughout this study. A first draft of this dissertation was read by Professors John G. Gurley and Melvin W. Reder, and their suggestions resulted in significant improvements of several parts of the text. Furthermore, Professor Paul A. David gave me many extremely helpful comments as did members of the very stimulating Abramovitz — David graduate seminar in economic history at Stanford University.

Of the many student members of this seminar, special thanks go to Warren Sanderson with whom I had numerous discussions both on some of the specific topics of this study as well as general problems of historical economic-demographic interactions from which I benefited enormously. Yoram Weiss read a first draft of Chapter V and suggested several improvements therein. Juul Bjerke of the Norwegian Central Bureau of Statistics was very helpful in making available some of the results, partly unpublished, of his empirical work on historical economic growth in Norway. Mrs. Udbjørg did an excellent job in typing this draft. Last, but not least, my wife Nina drew all the charts and otherwise supported me wholeheartedly throughout the undertaking of this study.

The major financial support for the research came from a grant from The Norwegian Science Foundation (NAVF); further funds and facilities were provided by the Research Center in Economic Growth, Stanford University. Furthermore, Stanford University provided a generous amount of computer time. I am in debt to all concerned. However, I retain sole responsibility for the remaining deficiencies and errors contained in this study.

TABLE OF CONTENTS

x

LIST OF ILLUSTRATIONS

Chart   Page

CHAPTER I

INTRODUCTION

> "The position we shall take is that
> the population variable is of impor-
> tance, and that it can be properly
> understood and evaluated only if it
> is examined in the light of an endog-
> enous variable."
>
> H. Leibenstein.
> Economic Backwardness and Economic
> Growth
> Chapter 10, p. 148.
> New York: Science Editions, 1963.

Most students interested in population problems will probably

agree that the course of economic development, either past, present or

future, may be bound up with changes in the size, composition and mobil-

ity of the population of a region or nation. Such interaction between

demographic and economic variables may be studied from many points of

view and at various levels of sophistication. One may, for example, as-

sume that the rate of economic growth is exogenously given and study its

impact on various aspects of population growth, and vice versa. A more

sophisticated approach would be to construct and empirically test models

where both categories of variables are determined endogenously. In addi-

tion, there is the time dimension. One may be primarily interested in

the long run interaction between economic and demographic variables. Con-

versely, one may prefer to focus on these relationships in the shorter

run, e.g. over cycles of various length.

Theoretical and empirical analysis of the interaction between demographic and economic variables during the process of economic growth, either historical or present, appears, however, to be a relatively neglected field of study. One reason may be that the study of economic demography today lies within an academic "no-man's land" between several recognized disciplines but not wholly within any one. Demographers, economists, historians and sociologists have, at one point or another, made contributions to our present stock of knowledge regarding demographic and socio-economic interrelations. In section I-1 I will limit myself to a brief survey of some of the economic-demographic literature that the present study attempts to build on. In section I-2 I proceed to outline the aim and scope of this monograph.

I-1. A Brief Survey of Economic-Demographic Literature

1.1. The Population Variable in Economic Theory

In the days of Malthus and Ricardo, the population variable occupied a central position within economic theory. In the classical growth model the rate of growth of population was postulated to be an endogenous variable being some function of the level of wages. A central question asked by the classisists was, for example: what is the long run relationship betw the rate of growth of population and the level of wages? Or, translated into modern terminology: assuming that some steady-state growth solution exists, what are the properties of such a solution regarding population growth and the level of wages? The answer, of course, depends on the exact specification of the various functions that make up

the specific model employed. One possibility is to arrive at the so-
called iron law of wages. If, in the Malthusian spirit, the supply of
population (labor) is perfectly elastic at a certain real wage corresponding to subsistence, the population grows at whatever rate will keep
the wage at this level.

It is probably fair to say that the main contribution of economic
theorists since that time regarding the theory of economic-demographic
interrelationships has been to reformulate and modify the basic classical
propositions in the more rigorous language of modern economics. In models
appearing almost simultaneously in the 1950's induced population changes
were admitted, the central hypothesis being that the rate of growth of
population (labor) is an increasing function of the real wage or income
per head. One can then proceed to ask much the same long run questions
as some of the classical economists were concerned with. The answer, once
more, depends on the exact specifications of the population, saving and
investment, production, technical progress and distribution of income
functions that make up the specific model in question. In the economic
development literature a much asked question has been: if an economy is
in a state of low-level (Malthusian) equilibrium that is stable to small
disturbances but not to large ones, what would it take for an economy to
escape from such a "low-level equilibrium" trap?

Such models where the rate of growth of population (the labor force)
is a variable may provide the empirical researcher with insight as to the
working of economic influences on mortality and fertility. The original
work of Malthus, for example, has had a strong impact on work done in

historical demography.[1]   However, regarding the neo-Malthusian literature
in this respect, the assessment of Hahn and Mattews is that: "The population functions used in the more recent literature provide a more sophisticated treatment of this, though they are still for the most part too
simplified to bear any close resemblance to reality; the main value of the
models in this respect is thus illustrative." [A18], pp. 25-26.[2] This
work has, furthermore, had little impact on growth models that deal, implicitly or explicitly, with the advance of developed or mature economies.[3]

1.2. The Demographers

Theoretical work on population has, of course, been carried out by
many non-economists, notably the demographers. Modern formal demography
may be regarded as a branch of probability theory and mathematical statistics, and the kind of theoretical mathematical models developed by the
late A. J. Lotka and others serve as a basis for much of the statistical
work done in pure demography. According to one Norwegian authority in the
field: "This field of study has as its purpose, in the first analysis, to
provide a statistical description of demographic events and their changes
without attempting to construct all-encompassing theories of population

[1]See for example Ohlin [B55] and Glass and Eversley [B24] and the
references contained in these books. See also Chapter III below.

[2]For more details on this literature, see Hahn and Mattews, ibid.,
especially sections I.6 and II.2.

[3]Professor Johansen, for example, considers population changes to
be exogenously determined in his multisectoral growth model arguing that:
"For an economy having already reached a relatively high standard of living I find this a realistic assumption." [B22], p. 21.

like the 'Malthusians' do." Hoem [B28], p. 2.[4] (My translation.) However, since the demographers are ultimately interested in why for example the fertility, mortality and the mobility of a population change over time, they have constructed theories in order to account for such changes. One such line of development is the application of the theory of stochastic probability models to demographic phenomena. A case in point is the use of the Markov process to analyze fertility, mortality and migration. See for example Kelley and Weiss [A22] and Parzen [B56] and the references contained therein. However, the assessment of Kelley and Weiss regarding such developments is that: "The popularity of the Markov model is derived from its appealing simplicity in describing dynamic processes, from the availability of data required for empirical analysis, and from its focus on the results, as distinct from the causes of social and economic change." ibid., p. 280. This examplifies, then, the general absence of economic and other social variables from much of demographic theory.[5] Thus, while economic theorists for the most part either exclude the population variable from their models or postulate it to be solely a function of economic variables, most of the work going on in demographic theory is void of economic content. Despite this fact, many of the concepts and measures developed within the field of demography has influenced empirical work on economic-demographic relationships.

---

[4]For a recent introduction to modern mathematical demography, see for example Keyfitz [B36].

[5]In Chapter V below, I will briefly illustrate the use of a simple Markov model in the analysis of migration and compare it with economic models.

1.3. Some Empirical-Historical Studies

Many empirical studies have focused on the interrelationships between demographic and socio-economic variables in the shorter run. The time dimension has often been fluctuations or cycles of various length. An early study by the Norwegian clergyman and sociologist Eilert Sundt, appearing more than a hundred years ago, focused on the observed long cycles in pre-industrial births and marriages. His theory was simple and based on the demographic concept of the "generation." Since the age-distribution of marriages and births is heavily concentrated within the ages 20 to 35, a destabilized age-structure of a population, caused by for example shocks that frequently impinged upon a pre-industrial economy, would lead to "generation" cycles in births and marriages due to the different size of successive cohorts. There would, furthermore, be successive echo effects of such "bulge-generations." Sundt found empirical support for his contention using Norwegian demographic time series. See [B66]. His study has become a classic in the Scandinavian population literature where historical 25 to 35 year swings in demographic variables are referred to as Sundt-cycles.

Sundt's simple hypothesis relies entirely, except for an initial shock, on an endogenous demographic explanation of long waves in population. In the 1930's the German economist August Lösch observed the same phenomena in German historical demographic time series, and he, in the main, embraced Sundt's explanation of them. See [A27], especially p. 653. Lösch then went one step further and maintained that these population cycles were one of the main causes of fluctuations in economic phenomena in Germany.

He argued that relatively rapid population growth would stimulate aggre-

gate demand by increasing the demand for housing. Secondly, increased

supply of labor would reduce cost of production.[6]

Some of the same effects of fluctuations in population growth on

economic phenomena have been elaborated upon in the largely American long

swing literature of the 1950's and 1960's. Professor Kuznets stresses

the role of population growth in generating waves in "population sensi-

tive" and "other" capital formation [B42], chap. 7. Professor Abramovitz

emphasizes the importance of population growth both as a source of addi-

tions to the labor supply and of demand for certain kinds of new capital

goods. He, furthermore, regards: "... population change and labor force

change, both in the aggregate and in their geographic distribution, not

as wholly autonomous phenomena, but as partly responsive to economic de-

velopments themselves;" [A2], p. 350. However, the self-generating demo-

graphic mechanism is largely absent from the American long swing litera-

ture. This is stated explicitely in a recent article by Professor Easter-

lin who argues regarding the U.S. experience that: "Fluctuations in demo-

graphic variables have typically arisen from movements in immigration or

the 'rate' components of change rather than from an echo effect of a

surge in births, operating through the aging and mortality component.

Such demographic fluctuations were induced by, rather than initiated,

---

[6]"It is natural that business leaders should take courage again
when a great increase in population guarantees them cheap labor and a
reliable extension of markets, especially for buildings and machinery."
[A27], pp. 657-658.

changes in economic activity, although in turn they had important feed-back effects." [A14], pp. 1085-86.[7]

It is quite clear that age-structure fluctuations may arise from several other reasons than echo effects of a surge in births, e.g., heavy spurts of immigration or emigration. This is demonstrated in an impor-tant recent paper by Kelly who shows that variations in the age structure derive from a large number of causes and are widely experienced empirical phenomena. He concludes that: "Age-specific demographic long swings are manifested in a variety of conditions: in regions of heavy emigra-tion; in regions ravaged by internal or by international war; in regions with and without a substantial demographic shock; and in historical or contemporary settings." [A21], p. 656.[8] Kelley, furthermore, argues that swings in the age structure of the total population may interact with micro-economic life-cycle responses regarding labor force partici-pation, demand for separate housing, and allocation of income between saving and consumption to influence swings in economic performance in the aggregate. This is an elaboration and clarification of the original Löschian view. Thus opinion on these matters seem to run in 30-year cycles of their own.

The long cycle or long swing literature singles out many pertinent

---

[7]In his recently published book, Easterlin's work and main ana-lytical views are set forth in more detail. See [B16]. This book con-tains a comprehensive bibliography of the work that has been carried out regarding long swings in economic and demographic growth in the U.S. and many other nations.

[8]This conclusion is based on a comprehensive empirical investiga-tion of historical and contemporary material in 14 different regions and nations. Ibid., pp. 645-55.

points of interaction between demographic and economic phenomena both in an historical and a contemporary setting. And in this respect it is, in many ways, much more realistic and empirically relevant than what I referred to as the purely theoretical literature above. However, much work remains to be done regarding the explicit formulation and empirical testing of many of the specific hypotheses set forth regarding such economic-demographic interrelationships. The models suggested are formulated in the oral tradition, and, for the most part, the empirical methodology has been the graphical comparison of (peaks and troughs in) time series which cannot rigorously establish the existence of statistically significant causality between economic and demographic variables. This may be one reason why some of the issues, for example regarding the "ultimate causes" of long swings, are not yet completely resolved.[9]

In recent years, however, empirical work on economic-demographic interactions has increasingly utilized econometric techniques. Most of these studies have been, to my knowledge, partial in character, i.e., the focus has been mainly on the economic influences on fertility, migration, etc. For such cross-section studies using econometric methodology, see Adelman [A3] and Weintraub [A42]. An example of time series analysis is a study by Silver [A33].

---

[9]There are, to be sure, other unresolved issues, for example regarding the "cyclic" interpretation of long swings and the extent to which some of the smoothing procedures employed in the empirical work themselves are chiefly responsible for cyclical movements. On these and related questions, the reader is referred to Adelman [A4].

I-2. The Aim and Scope of the Present Study

My purpose is to set up a number of hypotheses regarding economic-demographic interactions, manifestly in the form of simple aggregate models, and subject them to statistical tests, applying the methods of the new economic history, on the basis of available and created empirical information. The questions asked are partially influenced, if only indirectly, by developments in economic and demographic theory, partially by some of the issues raised in the long swing literature and quantitative economic history generally, and some have been created ad hoc.

The scope of the inquiry will be confined largely to the questions of the economic impact on demographic developments in Norway before 1940. The choice of Norway may be defended on several grounds other than the nationality of the author. First of all, relatively accurate demographic time series extending back more than 200 years have recently been complemented by empirical research carrying Norwegian national accounting figures back to 1865 in addition to providing new evidence regarding economic growth even before that time.[10] And while a largely descriptive survey of Norwegian historical demographic developments exists, no one, to my knowledge, has attempted to relate these analytically to the evidence we now have regarding Norwegian economic growth. Secondly, the study has been undertaken with the hope that the relative abundance of empirical evidence combined with the application of econometric techniques may throw new light on questions regarding historical-economic causes of population growth.

---

[10]The pre-1865 demographic data has recently been revised due to empirical research by Drake [B14].

One limitation of this study is that economic conditions for the most part will be assumed to be exogenously determined for the purpose of the analysis. Thus the models set forth are partial in character disregarding current feedback effects from demographic to economic variables. Past effects will be partially taken into consideration by entering for example the age-structure of the population as a predetermined variable. Indeed, a more sophisticated approach to the general problem of demographic-economic interaction would be to construct and empirically test full-fledged macro-models where both sets of factors are determined endogenously or "within the system." Since, to my knowledge, such an ambitious task has not yet been undertaken, it is hoped that the less ambitious objective briefly set forth above is still sufficiently interesting to yield a positive rate of return. But this, of course, is something the reader has to judge for himself.

Having made these introductory remarks, I proceed to briefly outline the plan of this inquiry. Chapter II will be partially devoted to a description of the long term trends and long swings in Norwegian demographic and economic growth before 1940. This is meant to serve partly as a means of familiarizing the non-Norwegian reader with the setting of our problem, and partly as a source of factual information to which explicit and implicit references can be made throughout the rest of the study. In the last two sections of this chapter I proceed to ask to what extent economic developments can account for some of the more marked changes in the long run trend of deaths and births.

Chapter III is devoted to an econometric analysis of the determinants of aggregate births and marriages in Norway before 1865, when internal and external migration was still of small quantitative significance. Thus the object of this chapter in effect becomes the successful prediction of births and marriages in a closed, pre-industrial population.

A second major objective of the dissertation is the explanation of the massive emigration from Norway that took place after 1865. In the period after the United States Civil War and up to World War I, Norway lost well over 40 percent of her natural increase, the highest national per capita figure recorded during this time period save that for Ireland. In Chapter IV I shall describe some of the relevant characteristics of the Norwegian overseas emigrants. Most of the characteristics of migrants which are significant from my point of view are more or less closely related to the labor market. The topic of this chapter was considered sufficiently interesting to be included, but, what is more important, the results are needed to support some of the assumptions made in the following chapter.

Perhaps the most important and most elaborate part of my study will be presented in Chapter V. The purpose of the chapter is to inquire about the economic and demographic causes of Norwegian labor emigration, and the examination is carried out with the help of an econometric model constructed more in the spirit of permanent income theories than in the wage differential approach. My basic migration hypothesis states that the propensity to migrate is in the long run a function of expected income relatives and the supply of young potential migrants. The short run adjustment of such regional disequilibrium will be dependent on the short run cost of moving. This model explains yearly Norwegian emigration to the United States between 1870 and 1914 very well. Furthermore, it can account for both the short and long cycles and the trend in yearly unsmoothed emigration series. Specifically, it is found that all of the predetermined variables predict long swings in Norwegian aggregate labor emigration — but with different timing. This conclusion rests on the use of the regression estimates to compute predicted overseas emigration due to one (or several) of the explanatory variables holding the rest constant at their means. Thus the actual observed long swing pattern in historical Norwegian emigration is due to all of the independent variables acting simultaneously on the endogenous variable; it is not caused by one single economic or demographic factor.

Finally, Chapter VI consists of a brief discussion of suggestions for further research in view of the major findings of the present study.

CHAPTER II

SECULAR TRENDS AND LONG SWINGS IN DEMOGRAPHIC

AND ECONOMIC GROWTH 1740—1940

> "..., I shall not be arguing that Kuz-
> nets cycles never existed — that this
> generalization about the form that
> growth used to assume in the United
> States and elsewhere was misconceived.
> I simply contend that it is a form of
> growth which belonged to a particular
> period in history and that the eco-
> nomic structure and institutions which
> imposed that form on the growth pro-
> cess have evolved, or been changed,
> into something different. My purpose
> is to try to guard the integrity and
> usefulness of the Kuznets-cycle hypoth-
> esis for interpreting development in
> the United States, Canada and Western
> Europe from about the 1840's to 1914
> by shielding it from an inappropriate
> confrontation with the different form
> which the growth process in these coun-
> tries is taking, and is likely to take,
> in the contemporary world."
>
> Moses Abramovitz.
> "The Passing of the Kuznets Cycle"
> Economica, New Series, Vol. XXV,
> No. 140 (November, 1968), p. 349.

II-1. Introduction

The present chapter is a review of the main features of the trends
and long swings in Norwegian demographic and economic growth between 1740
and 1940. A comprehensive new Norwegian economic history of the whole
period remains to be written. I have therefore attempted to give a com-

pact survey of demographic and economic growth during these two hundred years from the point of view of quantitative economic history. Some of the underlying sources and data may be little known, at least to economists. The present chapter may therefore have some merit in its own right. However, the main purpose of this review is to provide the readers who are largely unfamiliar with Norwegian economic history for the period before World War II with background material for a better appraisal of the analysis that will be attempted in subsequent chapters.

In Section II-2, the long run growth in additions to aggregate domestic population and its sub-components will be set forth. Section II-3 provides a brief summary of the Norwegian economic growth experience between 1740 and 1940. It is argued that Norway experienced considerable economic growth during the fifty years following the Napoleonic wars. This was accomplished largely, but not exclusively, through advances made in agriculture in a non-industrial economy.

The following period between 1865 and World War II is one of industrialization and structural transformation of the Norwegian economy. Norway participated actively in the opening up of the Atlantic economic community during these years, exporting labor along with goods and services and importing capital during part of the period. It is hypothesized that some of these developments may be systematically related to the long swings in economic growth that, at least before World War I, were in large measure inverse to those experienced by the economy of the United States.

Finally, in Section II-4 I ask, if only in a preliminary way, to what extent economic factors can account for some of the more marked

secular changes observed in Norwegian population growth.

II-2. Demographic Developments

2.1. The Rate of Growth of Aggregate Domestic Population

Since there are long swings of wide amplitude in the rate of

growth of aggregate domestic population measured as a rate per thousand

of mean domestic population, the underlying trends can best be discerned

if we attempt to date these swings and take averages for the periods

marked off by them. Each average represents a level in which the fluc-

tuations that constitute a swing have been canceled out, and the move-

ment of these averages should reveal the characteristics of the underly-

ing trend. These are exhibited in Table II-1.[1] See also Charts II-1

and II-2.

The average yearly growth of additions to domestic Norwegian popu-

lation varied widely between 1741 and 1940. During the first two long

swings, spanning roughly the eighteenth century, population grew at the

---

[1]Since there is no secure technique for describing these swings
accurately, it is not always easy to establish the precise dates of
their peaks and troughs. The use of single-year dates in Table II-1 may
suggest greater precision than is intended here. It may have been preferable to determine the peaks and troughs of the long swings from the
data for quinquennia rather than single years. But this procedure would
have complicated the calculation of average values for nonoverlapping
periods. The major conclusions suggested by Table II-1 would not, however, be affected by such modifications in the dating procedure. Note,
furthermore, that I refrain from arguing that these swings are "cyclic"
or entirely self-generating in nature.

fairly moderate average yearly rate of between 4 and 6 per thousand of mean population. This trend rate of growth accelerated sharply during the following two swings reaching a yearly average exceeding 10 per thousand during the middle of the nineteenth century, a doubling of the growth rate experienced during the previous century. The growth of domestic population then falls off to an intermediate level during the succeeding three long swings only to reach a trend rate of growth during the years preceding World War II comparable to the first long swing for which we have data.

To gain further insight into this growth pattern we turn to a brief review of the major underlying components of additions to domestic population, namely, births, deaths, and emigration.

2.2. Growth of the Underlying Components of Domestic Population Growth

2.2.1. Births. The average yearly rate of growth of births per thousand of mean population during the long swings marked off in aggregate domestic population growth is exhibited in column 1 of Table II-1. This measure is, of course, called the crude birth rate.[2] Two impressions emerge. First, during the first six long swings or roughly up to the beginning of the twentieth century the crude birth rate stays remark-

---

[2]If B is the total number of live births among residents in a community during a calendar year, and P is the average number of persons living in that community during the year, then the crude birth rate, CBR, simply is $\frac{B}{P} \cdot k$, where k is a constant taken as one thousand in this case. The definitions of the crude death and emigration rates are analogous where the numerator in the latter two cases refer to the total number of deaths and emigrants respectively.

TABLE II-1

YEARLY AVERAGE VOLUME OF
BIRTHS, DEATHS, NATURAL INCREASE, EMIGRATION
AND ADDITIONS TO DOMESTIC POPULATION
BETWEEN TROUGH TO TROUGH
LONG SWINGS IN ADDITIONS TO DOMESTIC POPULATION,
1741-1940*

	(1)	(2)	(3)	(4)	(5)
Time Period	Crude Birth Rate	Crude Death Rate	Rate of Natural Increase (per 1000 of Mean Pop.)= Column 1 Minus Column 2	Crude Emigration Rate	Rate of Addition to Domestic Pop. = Column 3 Minus Column 4
1741-1773	31.19**	26.75	4.44	–	4.44
1773-1809	30.21	24.69	5.52	–	5.52
1809-1839	30.85	20.94	9.91	–	9.91
1839-1869	31.28	17.98	13.30	2.79	10.51
1869-1882	30.58	17.12	13.46	6.74	6.72
1882-1903	30.26	16.40	13.86	7.01	6.85
1903-1927	24.48	13.23	11.25	4.68	6.57
1927-1940	15.99	10.57	5.42	0.97	4.45

* Sources of data: 1740-1865: [B14], Appendix Tables 5 and 7, pp. 184-195.

    1865-1940: [G16], Table 14, pp. 43-44.

** (All figures are expressed as rates per 1000 of mean domestic population.)

CHART II-1 INCREASE IN POPULATION PER 1000 OF MEAN POPULATION 1735-1835 NORWAY

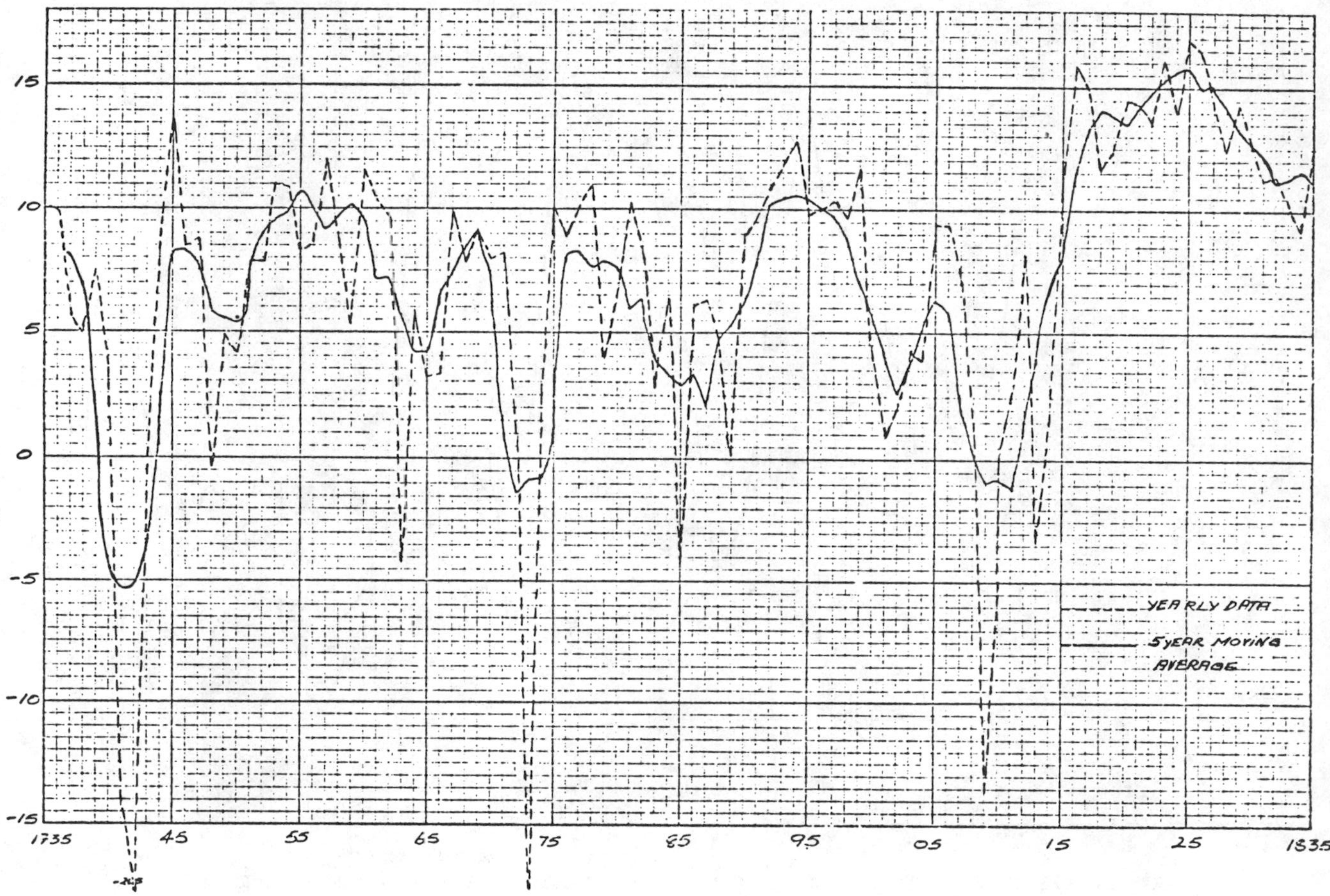

CHART II-2   INCREASE IN DOMESTIC POPULATION PER 1000 OF MEAN POPULATION 1836-1936   NORWAY

5 Year Moving Average

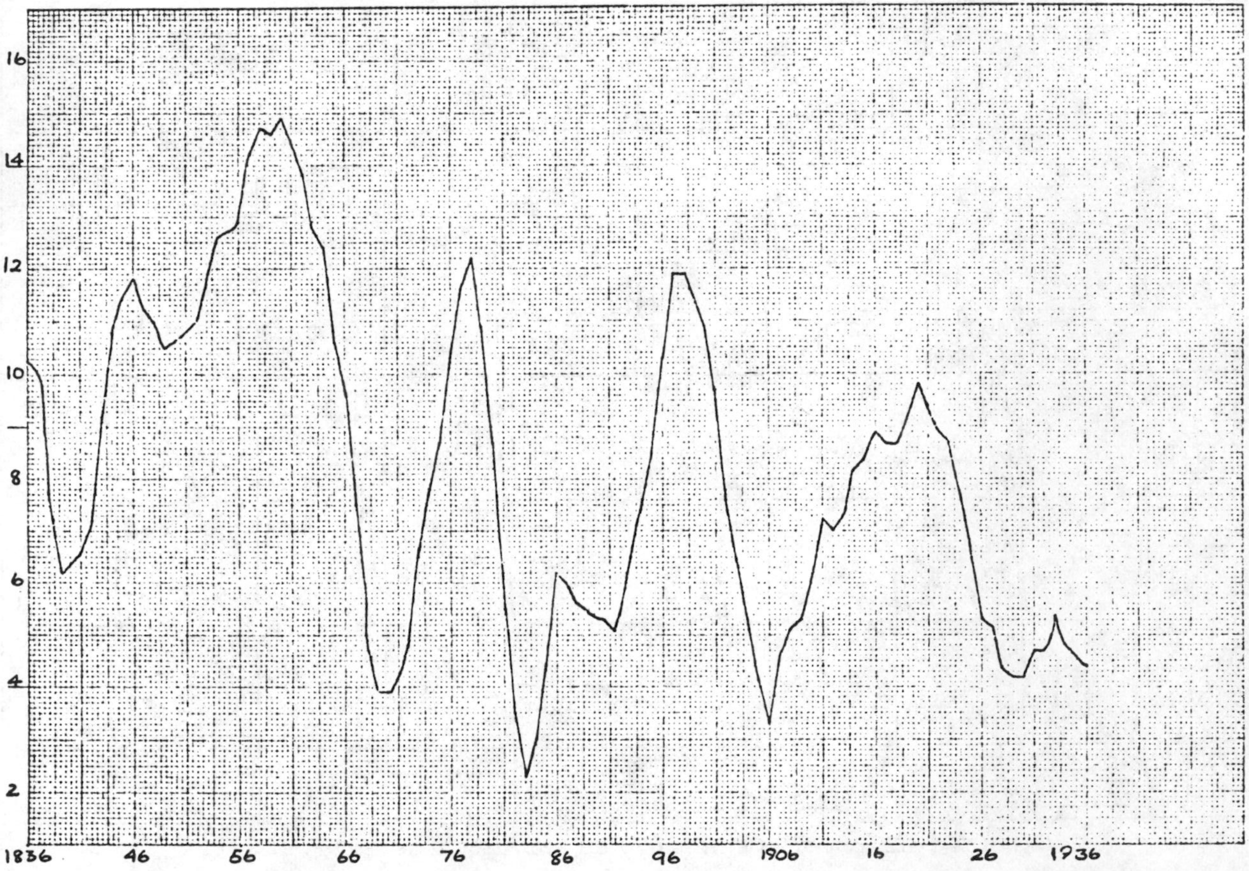

ably constant, varying between the relatively narrow limits of 30.2 and
31.2. Secondly, during the following forty years the birth rate falls
to roughly half of its former long run level, indicating a marked and
abrupt change in the secular trend.

It is clear that the observed long run stability in the crude
birth rate could come about by several combinations of events. The measure is influenced not only by the number of births, B, in a community,
but also by the composition of the total population, P. Thus, if the
number of births and the proportion of (married) females at the reproductive ages in the total population remain constant, the crude birth rate
will remain constant. However, such a constancy may also result from
opposite movements in B and the proportion of (married) females capable
of reproduction in P. To normalize for this possibility one may compute
the general (marital) fertility rate defined simply as the ratio of total
(legitimate) births to total (married) female population at the reproductive ages. However, if the number of births vary markedly with age
within the range of effective reproductive ages, normally set at fifteen
to forty-five years of age for females, a preferable measure would be
age-specific birth or fertility rates.[3] Such fertility measures are set
forth in Table II-2.

---

[3]If nBx is the number of children born to (married) mothers between ages x and $x+n$ in a community during a year, and $nFPx$ is the
average number of (married) females between ages x and $x+n$ living in
that community during the same year, then the age-specific birth rate,
$nASBRx$, is $= \frac{nBx}{nFPx} \cdot k$, where k is a constant again taken to be one thousand. If $x=$fifteen years and $n=$thirty years, $30ASBR15$ is equal to the
definition of the general (marital) fertility or birth rate given above.

TABLE II-2

FERTILITY RATES BY AGE OF MOTHER.
SELECTED DATES 1769-1965

A. BIRTHS PER 1000 WOMEN

(1)	(2)	(3)
Annual Average	Women 21-50	Women 15-44
1765-69	154	
1796-1800	148	
1860-65	154	
1899-1900	151	133
1932-35	70	61
1961-65		89

B. LEGITIMATE BIRTHS PER 1000 EVERMARRIED AND MARRIED WOMEN

(1)	(2)	Married Women						
		(3)	(4)	(5)	(6)	(7)	(8)	(9)
Annual Average	Evermarried Women 15-49	15-44	15-19	20-24	25-29	30-34	35-39	40-44
1765-69	244							
1796-1800	222							
1860-65	230							
1899-1900	235	305	593	485	382	333	264	159
1930-31	124	161	694	374	237	163	115	61
1959-62		134	555	330	215	133	71	26

Data Sources: Panel A, col. 2: 1765-1865 computed from data in [B14], p. 76; 1899-1900 and 1932-35 computed from data in [G20], Tables 16 and 20.
Panel A, col. 3: [G20], Table 26, p. 50.
Panel B, col. 2: 1765-1865 computed from data given in [B14], Table 42; 1899-1900 and 1930-31 computed from data in [G20], Tables 16 and 20.
Panel B, columns 3-9: [B3], Table 63, p. 112.

Two impressions stand out regarding the long run trend in the general birth or fertility rate. First, the general fertility rate remains remarkably stable around the selected census dates between 1769 and 1900. The same long run stability is found regarding marital fertility during the same time period. Thus, the secular constancy in the crude birth rate that was observed up to the end of the 19th century seems to be a reflection of a constancy of fertility, both general and marital, over the period.

Secondly, Table II-2 reveals that the general birth rate fell rapidly after 1900. This fall is accompanied by a comparable fall in general marital fertility; e.g., the number of legitimate births per 1000 married women between the ages of 15 and 44 fell rapidly from an average level of 305 in 1899-1900 to almost half this number, or 161, in 1930-31. Thus the fall in the crude birth rate during the first thirty years of the 20th century must have been mainly caused by a fall in general (marital) fertility. Furthermore, this fall in turn can be traced to declines in the fertility in five of the six underlying age-groups, but in differing degree. The rates for the three oldest age-groups, 30-34, 35-39 and 40-44, respectively, fall proportionally substantially more than the total. Fertility of mothers in their twenties also declines markedly, but by much less than the older age-groups. And the youngest age-group consisting of those 15 to 19 years of age exhibits a rising age-specific birth rate. This sharp fall in fertility continued, with a brief interruption after World War II, into the 1960's. Thus the period around the turn of the century marked off a beginning of a sustained long term downward movement in age-specific fertility, especially among married women above thirty years of age.

2.2.2. Deaths. Long swing averages of the crude death rate are set forth in column 2 of Table II-1. This measure of mortality falls from one successive swing to the next during the entire two-hundred-year period. However, this fall in the long run level does not proceed evenly. There is a marked acceleration in the downward movement during the sixty years marked off as the third and fourth swing, the decrease in the yearly long swing average being almost 4 and 3 per thousand respectively. The crude death rate decreases by less than two points during the succeeding thirty-four years only to, once more, accelerate its downward movement in the twentieth century.

The acceleration in the fall of the crude death rate observed after the Napoleonic wars is probably to some extent associated with the disappearance of the occasional "dismal peaks" that can be observed in deaths before this time.[4] To throw more light on this question it would, once more, have been desirable to have data on deaths distributed by age. Specifically we would have liked to study the age-specific impact of mortality during the years exhibiting abnormally high crude death rates. Such in-

---

[4] These peaks can be seen in Chart II-3. Extremely high values of deaths per thousand of population occurred in the following years: 1741: 40.8, 1742: 52.2, 1773: 47.5, 1809: 35.9. 1809 is the last year with a crude death rate above 30. If we exclude these extreme values from our calculations of long swing averages, these become: 1743-1772 (excluding 1741, 1742 and 1773 from the first swing): 24.75. 1774-1808 (excluding 1773 and 1809 from the second long swing): 22.99. 1810-1839 (excluding 1809 from the third swing): 20.44. Thus, if we disregard disaster years, a picture of a more even decline during the period 1741-1839 is revealed.

formation is unavailable. However, due to recent research by Drake [B14], some evidence regarding the first decades of the 19th century should be briefly mentioned.

In 1801, a year in which the crude death rate equalled 27.4 in Norway which was the highest for any year between 1789 and 1809, some 46 boys and 43 girls under 10 years of age died for every 1000 in that age group. In the same year, the age-specific figures for the age-group 41—50 were 17.9 and 15.3 per 1000 respectively. Thus, during a year of a relatively high (but not quite dismal) crude death rate, the age-specific death rates below 10 years of age were almost three times as high as those of the age-group 41 to 50. Furthermore, if one compares age-specific mortality figures for the first decade of the 19th century with those for the period 1816—1840, it is clear that the numbers for the group below 10 years of age fall proportionally much more than for the older age groups. There is some indication, then, that child mortality was proportionally much higher during years of relatively high crude death rates before 1815, and that it fell proportionally much more than age-specific mortality above 10 years of age after this date.[5]

Data on infant mortality, i.e., deaths of infants aged 0-1 per 1000 live births, become available only as late as the 1830's. The figures show that infant mortality rates one hundred years ago were still extremely high compared to more recent figures. During the time period 1841-1870 more than one out of every ten children born died before reaching the age

---

[5]For more details, the reader is referred to Drake, op. cit., especially pp. 45-49.

of one on the average each year.[6] The secular decline we observe in infant mortality resembles to a certain extent that in the crude death rate. The slow fall during the last sixty years of the nineteenth century is followed by a marked acceleration in the downward level at the turn of the century. The acceleration in the secular fall in infant mortality was more pronounced than that experienced in total deaths. Between 1886-1905 and 1926-1940 the average yearly number of infant deaths fell from 93 to 45 per thousand live births, a halving of the infant mortality rate in less than half a century. In this same time span the relative decrease of mortality in the ages 1 to 14 was even more dramatic, especially in the age group 1 to 4 years. On the other hand, the decline of the age-specific death rates between 15 and 69 occurred much more slowly, and mortality in the oldest age group changed hardly at all.

We may therefore conclude that the acceleration in the secular decline in total deaths that occurred approximately around the turn of the nineteenth century was accompanied, and to a large extent caused, by very dramatic declines in the deaths of infants and children below fifteen years of age. Deaths in the older age groups, on the other hand, declined more slowly and less uniformly.[7]

---

[6]This figure is comparable to the infant mortality rate observed in Sweden during the same period. The Swedish data extends back into the eighteenth century, and the average yearly infant mortality figure for Sweden for the period 1751-1800 is 202 per thousand live births. See Gille [A15], page 36. Thus, if one is willing to extrapolate the Norwegian data backwards on the basis of the Swedish experience, the infant mortality rate observed in the middle of the nineteenth century was, very roughly, half that observed in the latter half of the eighteenth century.

[7]More details for the period after 1856 are given in [B2].

2.2.3. Emigration. The first recorded emigration in modern times occurred in 1825 when fifty-two persons set out in a small sailing ship for the U.S.[8] Emigration on a yearly scale started towards the end of the 1830's and grew to a yearly average of close to 3 per thousand during the fourth long swing in aggregate population growth. During the two swings following the U.S. Civil War this trend average more than doubled. This was the highest recorded per capita emigration figure from any country during this time period save Ireland. The level of migration falls off during the subsequent long swing only to become very insignificant after the onset of legal restrictions to overseas migration in the 1920's.

We are now ready to briefly assess how the underlying components contributed to the observed changes in the trend rate of growth of the aggregate domestic population in Norway 1741-1940. Firstly, the marked increase in the rate of natural increase in the nineteenth century as compared with the previous one was caused mainly by a falling death rate accompanied by a relatively constant birth rate. This acceleration in the rate of natural increase was largely confined to the sixty years following the Napoleonic wars. During the remainder of the nineteenth century natural increase in population remains at the level reached earlier. However, the average yearly rate of growth of additions to domestic population reaches a peak during the fourth long swing. Between the years

---

[8]Emigration refers to overseas migration. Data on Norwegian migration to Scandinavian and Continental European countries became available at a much later date. It was recorded to be very small in both directions and cancel each other. The nature of the overseas migration data will be discussed in more detail in Chapter IV.

1839 and 1869 this rate was above one percent per year, the highest sustained rate of domestic population growth in Norwegian history.

During the following three long swings mass emigration cuts heavily
into a relatively high rate of natural increase. In the course of these
fifty-seven years almost half of the natural addition to Norwegian population was lost through out-migration, thus causing aggregate domestic
population to grow at a rate which was intermediate between the low rates
of the eighteenth century and the much higher rates of the early nineteenth century.

Despite the cessation of this large out-migration stream towards
the end of the 1920's, population growth during the years prior to World
War II was almost identical to that experienced during the very first
long swing for which we have data. Although the death rate by now had
fallen to between one-half and one-third of its level in the mid-eigh-
teenth century, the extremely rapid fall in the birth rate caused aggregate domestic population growth to be similar to that experienced almost
two hundred years earlier.

2.3. The Rate of Growth of the Male and Female Population Between 20 and
       39 Years of Age. Long Swings in the Norwegian Population of Family
       Forming and Migratory Ages

Having accounted for the rate of growth of the aggregate domestic
Norwegian population, I now turn to the growth pattern of selected subgroups of this total, namely, those males and females between 20 and 39
years of age. These are the ages where people typically marry and have

most of their children, and where the mobility of a population is normally
the highest. The main purpose of this section is to show that there were
indeed pronounced long swings or Sundt-cycles in the growth of population
in these age-groups in Norway between 1801 and World War II.

The story starts with the last dismal peak in deaths around 1810
and the very high compensatory birth rates between 1816 and 1825, i.e.,
after the Napoleonic wars. See Chart II-3. The echo-effect of these
events is exhibited in Table II-3. Here we have computed the average annual rates of growth of males and females in family forming and migratory
ages. Before 1845 the figures refer to yearly growth rates between census
dates. See lines (1) to (3). After this time we can follow the average
yearly growth of quinquennial averages of these age-groups ten years apart.
The first echo-effect alluded to above can be seen in lines (3) and (4)
of Table II-3. Between 1835 and 1845 the male population between 20 and
29 years of age grew at an average rate of 3.5 percent per year, the highest figure recorded in our table. The respective number for females was
3.2 percent during the same decade. During the next time period this un-
usually large cohort was 10 years older. Thus from 1846/50 to 1856/60
the male and female age-groups 30 to 39 years of age swelled and grew at
the rate of 2.6 and 2.4 percent per year respectively.

This last development, in turn, contributed to an echo-effect regarding births. See Chart II-4. The crude birth rate rose markedly between the early 1840's and the late 1850's. Thus the age-group 20-29
grew rapidly, or around 1.5 percent per year, between 1866/70 and 1876/80,
and those aged 30 to 39 grew relatively rapidly during the following time

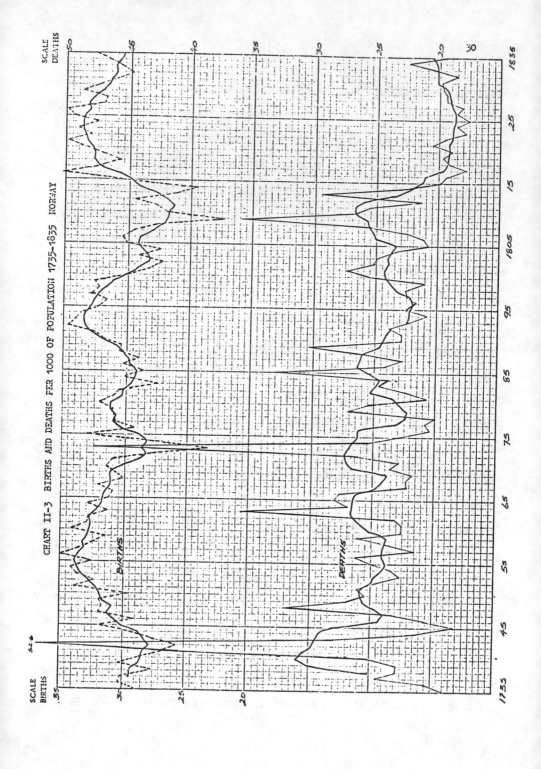

CHART II-3 BIRTHS AND DEATHS PER 1000 OF POPULATION 1755-1835 NORWAY

TABLE II-3

AVERAGE ANNUAL RATES OF GROWTH OF THE NORWEGIAN MALE AND
FEMALE POPULATION BETWEEN 20 AND 39 YEARS OF AGE
AS COMPARED WITH THE TOTAL POPULATION
1801-1936/40. Percent per year

| | MALES | | | FEMALES | | |
TIME PERIODS	MALES 20-29	MALES 30-39	ALL MALES	FEMALES 20-29	FEMALES 30-39	ALL FEMALES
(1) 1801-1825	1.1	1.1		0.9	0.7	
(2) 1825-35	-0.2	0.7		-0.2	0.7	
(3) 1835-45	3.5	0.03		3.2	-0.01	
(4) 1846/50-1856/60	0.1	2.6	1.3	0.6	2.4	1.3
(5) 1856/60-1866/70	0.3	-0.1	1.1	0.2	0.4	1.1
(6) 1866/70-1876/80	1.5	0.0	0.8	1.6	0.1	0.9
(7) 1876/80-1886/90	-0.7	0.8	0.4	0.0	1.1	0.7
(8) 1886/90-1896/1900	1.3	0.3	0.9	0.7	0.7	0.9
(9) 1896/1900-1906/10	0.4	0.9	0.7	0.7	0.7	0.8
(10) 1906/10-1916/20	2.5	1.4	1.0	1.6	1.2	0.9
(11) 1916/20-1926/30	1.2	1.7	0.8	1.1	1.7	0.7
(12) 1926/30-1936/40	1.4	2.3	0.58	0.7	1.5	0.4

Lines (1) to (3) computed from [G2], Table 20, pp. 234-37
Lines (4) to (12) computed from [G20], Table 18, pp. 38-41.

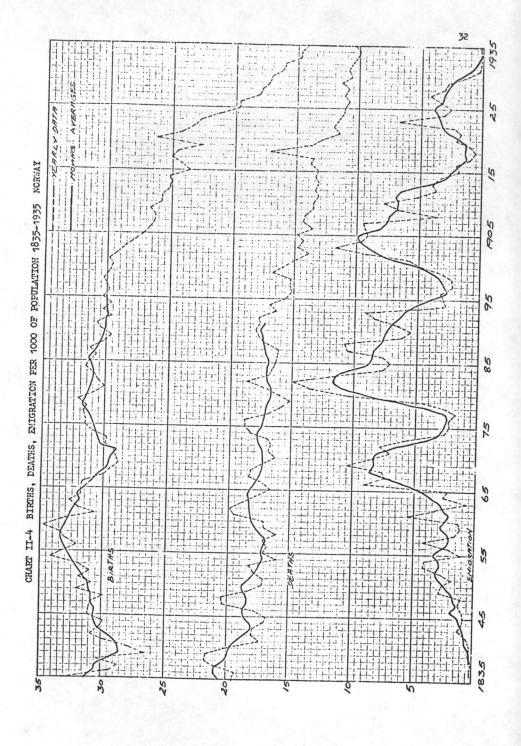

CHART II-4 BIRTHS, DEATHS, EMIGRATION PER 1000 OF POPULATION 1855-1935 NORWAY

period. Emigration now becomes a factor in addition to prior births. For example, during the years 1876/80-1886/90 overseas emigration was exceptionally heavy, and the stock of Norwegian males between 20 and 29 decreased markedly during these years while the stock of females in the same ages remained the same.

The subsequent long swings in the pattern of growth of Norwegian males and females in family forming and migratory ages is partly a result of damped echo-effects of births, partly a result of the long swings in emigration itself, and, after the end of the 19th century, partly a result of increasing survival ratios. For example, the relatively rapid growth of males between 20 and 29 between 1896/90 and 1896/1900 is partly the result of the birth pattern in the 1870's and the relatively low level of emigration during the period. After 1910 the level of emigration falls off, and the survival effect of falling mortality compensates for the falling level of births.

It has been shown that there were marked long swings or Sundt-cycles in the rate of growth of the Norwegian population between the ages of 20 and 39. Before the years of heavy overseas Norwegian emigration, these swings must have been mainly a reflection of compensatory peaks (and troughs) in births as Eilert Sundt told us more than a hundred years ago. After 1865 emigration became an additional factor. So did markedly rising survival probabilities after 1900. If we, furthermore, compare the growth pattern of the population in the family forming and migratory ages with that of the total or aggregate Norwegain population, we see that these differ markedly in most periods between 1801 and 1940, the rate of growth of the total population generally fluctuating much less. For an analysis of causes of, for example, births and migration it is clearly the former population category which is relevant as will be attempted to be shown in Chapters III, V and VI below. But also when it comes to the _impact_ of population growth _on_ economic variables such as the demand for housing, the supply of labor and the supply of personal saving, it may be very misleading to focus on the growth of aggregate population.

2.4. The Rural-Urban Distribution of Population

We now turn briefly to a review of how the Norwegian population was distributed between rural and urban areas throughout this period, and how this distribution changed over time. Such a review will have to rely heavily on the data provided by the official censuses since yearly data is largely unavailable. The relative numbers of rural and urban inhabitants are set forth in Table II-4.

It is clear that we have to face an index number problem when we attempt to compare the rural-urban distribution of a population over a time span of one hundred and sixty years. There are at least two problems which have to be faced. Firstly, administrative boundaries may change from one census to the next so that a change in the domestic distribution of population may occur even without any rural-urban migration or differences in natural increase. To try to adjust for boundary changes would be a major undertaking and is beyond the scope of this brief review. The figures in Table II-4 therefore refer to the boundaries existing in the years when the censuses were taken.

TABLE II-4

RURAL-URBAN DISTRIBUTION OF THE NORWEGIAN POPULATION
AT SELECTED CENSUS DATES 1769-1930

	(1)	(2)	(3)	(4)	(5)	(6)	(7)	(8)
Census Dates	% of Total Pop. RURAL DISTRICTS	% of Total Pop. RURAL AGGLOMERATIONS	Col.1 Minus Col.2	% of Total Pop. ADMINISTRATIVE TOWNS	Col.2 Plus Col.4 TOWNS & RURAL AGGLOMERATIONS	% of Total Pop. URBAN SETTLEMENTS	% of Total Pop. DISPERSED SETTLEMENTS	Average Yearly Change of Col.6 between Census Dates
1769	91.1*	-*	-*	8.9*	-*	-*	-*	-**
1801	91.2	-	-	8.8	-	-	-	-
1845	87.8	3.3	84.5	12.2	15.5	-	-	-
1865	84.4	3.9	80.5	15.6	19.5	-	-	-
1875	81.7	6.3	75.4	18.3	24.6	23.5	76.5	-
								0.39
1890	76.3	7.6	68.7	23.7	31.3	29.3	70.7	
								0.61
1900	72.0	7.7	64.3	28.0	35.7	35.4	64.6	
								0.30
1910	71.2	9.7	61.5	28.8	38.5	38.4	61.6	
								0.50
1920	70.4	15.6	54.8	29.6	45.2	43.4	56.6	
								0.25
1930	71.5	18.8	52.7	28.5	47.3	45.9	54.1	

* Figures in these columns refer to % of total population

** Figures in this column refer to yearly change in col.6 between census dates

<u>Sources of data</u>: Columns (1) - (5): [B2], Table 1, page 24
Columns (6), (7) : [B53], p. 73.

Secondly, and perhaps more importantly, as a country becomes increasingly industrialized some part of the population may be recorded as
living in rural areas while they are engaged in non-agricultural activities. Happily, some adjustment can be made to take account of this fact.
Since 1845 the number of people living in rural agglomerations has been
recorded separately in the censuses. And starting in 1875 we can draw
on previous work distinguishing between urban and dispersed settlements.
An urban settlement is defined as consisting of at least two hundred inhabitants where seventy-five percent or more of the working population
is engaged in industries other than agriculture and forestry.[9]

Where either one of these two criteria are not fulfilled, the population is characterized as living in a dispersed settlement. Thus a rural
agglomeration would be characterized as a dispersed settlement only if
more than one-fourth of its work force was engaged in agriculture or forestry. It turns out that the relative number of people that lived in
rural agglomerations and administrative towns was very close to the number that lived in urban settlements. Compare columns 5 and 6 in Table II-4.
Consequently the number of inhabitants in dispersed settlements was close
to the number we get by deducting the persons that lived in rural agglomerations from the total population characterized as rural. Compare columns 3 and 7.

From Table II-4 we see that in 1769 Norway was largely a traditional
rural society in which over nine out of every ten persons lived in rural

---

[9]For a detailed definition and discussion of this concept, see
Myklebost [B53], especially pages 46-48.

areas. Almost one hundred years later, on the eve of mass emigration, this picture had not changed radically. Less than twenty percent of the population resided in towns and rural agglomerations in 1865. A marked acceleration in urbanization took place during the succeeding sixty-five years. At the turn of the nineteenth century more than one-third of the population lived and worked in urban settlements, and in 1930, when the last wave of heavy emigration had come to a halt, the Norwegian population was approximately evenly distributed between urban and dispersed settlements. This redistribution of domestic population did not, however, proceed at an even pace from decade to decade. From column 6 in Table II-4 the average yearly changes between census dates of the relative number of people in urban settlements were computed and recorded in column 8. From this column it can be seen that urban settlement was especially rapid during the last decade of the nineteenth century and the second decade of the twentieth. These were decades of relatively low overseas emigration. Conversely, during the remaining three intercensal periods between 1875 and 1930 the urban influx proceeded at a slower pace. During these periods emigration was very high. Can we, then, establish a systematic relation between rural-urban migration and out-migration to overseas countries? We will briefly try to throw additional light on that question in Chapter IV below.

II-3. Economic Growth and Development

Fairly comprehensive figures on aggregate Norwegian economic growth
are now available starting in 1865. Before this time the primary statistical material is of much poorer quality and no attempts have been made
to arrive at national accounting measures. For the period before 1865 we
are therefore forced to rely on scattered quantitative figures referring
to individual industries in addition to qualitative accounts.

3.1. The Pre-1865 Period

3.1.1. Agriculture. The eighteenth century is a dark age as far
as agricultural statistics is concerned. Grains were the major crops
grown in a traditional subsistence setting. The only change of any consequence we know of during this period was the introduction of the potato
as a new crop. The potato came to Norway probably from England or Scot-
land in the 1750's but was not adopted on a major scale until the following century. A sharp increase in the cultivation of potatoes occurred
between the 1800's and the 1830's, and by 1835 the potato was a major
crop in Norway.[10]

A good deal of new land was broken during the decades following
the Napoleonic wars and Norway's gain of political independence from Denmark in 1814. According to an historical account by Steen, 128,000 decare
(equal to roughly 31,600 acres) of new agricultural land was taken into
use during the 1820's while 200,000 decare was broken during the follow-

---

[10]For a more detailed account of this development, see Drake [A11],
especially pages 115-123.

ing decade. These figures, to be sure, are not based on nationwide censuses. However, Steen claims that, if anything, they are on the low side and that a substantial amount of land clearing had taken place even before 1820.[11]

The first reasonably comprehensive quantitative information regarding Norwegian agriculture stems from a government survey taken in 1809. Information was allegedly gathered from every parish regarding the kind and amount of seed sown and the harvest both during a normal year and during that of 1809. The first official Norwegian census of agriculture was taken in connection with the population census in 1835 and was followed by similar nationwide counts in 1845, 1855 and 1865. Some of the main results of these are set forth in Table II-5.

Naturally, we would expect the quantities in this table to be understated, and in differing degrees. The later censuses are allegedly more accurate than the early ones for reasons well known. While the counts in 1809 and 1835 may understate the true quantities by 10 to 20 percent, the figures for 1855 and 1865 are probably much closer to their true values. Thus the increase between 1809 and 1855, for example, computed from the data in Table II-5 will be biased upwards. This should, of course, be kept in mind. However, even quite liberal allowances for such biases cannot change the major conclusions that emerge from an examination of these early agricultural figures.[12]

---

[11]See Steen [B64], especially p. 26. An English summary of this book can be found in Excerpta Historica Nordica, III.

[12]The nature and accuracy of these early agricultural censuses is discussed in detail in a very thorough and comprehensive study by Valen-Sendstad. See [B73], especially pp. 270-275 and pp. 336-338 and the references cited therein. See also [A5].

TABLE II-5

ROUGH INDICATORS OF INPUTS, OUTPUTS, AND OUTPUT PER
UNIT OF INPUT IN NORWEGIAN AGRICULTURE AT
SELECTED CENSUS DATES 1800-1865

	(1) Normal year before 1809	(2) 1835	(3) 1855	(4) 1865
A. INPUTS				
Seed (a) Corn and peas (hl)	334,000	380,000	555,000	551,000
(b) Potatoes (hl)	27,000	163,000	296,000	360,000
(c) = (a) + (b)	361,000	543,000	851,000	911,000
Labor (d) Agricultural Population	710,000	920,000	1,030,000	1,090,000
Area of Cultivated Farm Land				
(e) Corn and peas (decare)		1,286,523		1,851,444
(f) Potatoes (decare)		146,638		323,710
(g) Enrolled farms	79,000	105,000	128,000	148,000
B. OUTPUT				
(h) Gross harvest (hl)	1,520,000	3,336,000	6,096,000	6,155,000
C. OUTPUT PER UNIT OF INPUT				
(i) Harvest per unit of land (hl per decare)		2.32		2.83
(j) Harvest per member of agr. population (hl per head)	2.1	3.6	5.9	5.7
(k) Harvest per farm unit	19	32	47	42
(l) Average yield	4.2	6.1	7.1	6.7

(hl = hectolitres of barley. A hectolitre ≈ 2.75 bushels)

Data Sources: Lines a, b, c, d, g, and h: [B73]
Lines e and f: [G16], Table 42, p. 69.

The area of cultivated farmland continued to expand substantially after 1835. The recorded increase between the census in that year and 1865 is almost 750,000 decare. Thus farmland grew at the average yearly rate of 1.4 percent in this period. Even if we reduce this figure by 20 percent, the fact remains that new agricultural land was taken into use during this period at the rate of at least 200,000 decare per decade. This is comparable to the figures cited above regarding the period before 1835. Given the nature of agricultural production techniques in Norway in the first half of the 19th century, land, along with labor, must have been a major factor of production and source of potential capital formation at the time. Accordingly, such capital formation must have proceeded at a fairly impressive rate.

Turning to gross agricultural harvests, we see that it doubled roughly every 30 years between the first decade of the 19th century and 1865. Furthermore, our rather crude indicators of output per unit of input rose substantially during the same time period. As measured, output per member of the agricultural population almost tripled between 1809 and 1855. And even if we adjust the 1809 figure upwards quite liberally, it is probably fair to conclude that average harvest per person must at least have doubled during this time period. All the other indicators convey similar impressions of increased output per unit of input. Thus, as far as these figures go, they all indicate unmistakable advances in productivity in Norwegian agriculture during roughly the first half of the 19th century.

Other qualitative evidence from this period is clearly consistent

with such findings and points to marked technological change within the
agricultural sector. Valen-Sendstad concludes that: "In all the areas
where research was undertaken, the signs of transformation appeared.
This also resulted in an increased investment in agricultural machinery,
at times a substantial increase. Even though there might be various
levels in the tool-culture from one district to another, there was a
similar tendency in the general trend." [B73], p. 312.[13]

There are several specific developments underlying the general
picture of changing technology. Between 1800 and 1850 there was a distinct shift from the primitive wooden plough towards the more advanced
iron ploughs. In many places the iron plough had won universal recog-
nition, and in others the plough replaced the spade. One result was
that while the ploughing depth around 1800 had been around 4 inches,
the new machinery resulted in a standard depth around 6-8 inches fifty
years later. Harrow-tools continued throughout the early years of the
19th century to win new ground, and by the 1850's the threshing machine
had become a fairly common machine, at least on the larger farms. Finally, the spread of wheel implements, replacing the rope, basket and
pack as means of transportation led to substantial savings in labor costs.

---

[13]As already alluded to above, this book by Valen-Sendstad is by
far the most comprehensive and best documented piece of research on the
development and implementation of agricultural tools and techniques in
particular, and on the growth of Norwegian agriculture in general, between 1800-1850. Furthermore, his very careful empirical investigation,
which reveals a lot of new evidence, demonstrates fairly conclusively
that Norwegian agriculture developed happily in this time period. Thus,
previous accounts holding largely opposite views should probably be dis-
carded. For more details, see Valen-Sendstad, op. cit.

The rising of the tool-culture was no isolated phenomenon. The open-field system which had been prevalent in the 18th century began to disappear. In regions with a favorable market situation, the open-field system even on the home fields was in many places entirely given up before 1850. Thus it is clear that Norwegian agriculture experienced considerable technological progress between 1800 and the 1850's

At no time, however, was agricultural production sufficient to cover total domestic consumption. Between 1835 and 1865 imports of grain amounted to about forty percent of total consumption on the average, while the import figure for potatoes fluctuated between twenty-five and thirty percent.[14] How were these imports paid for? We now turn briefly to that question.

3.1.2. The Export Trades. From the seventeenth century onwards, some primitive industrial activities were incorporated into the economic structure in Norway. They were based on natural resources such as vast forests, easily available waterpower and some not very abundant mineral resources. A large number of small water-driven sawmills provided timber for export. England was the main buyer and probably the most important source of foreign exchange earnings in the eighteenth century. If the Napoleonic wars provided an impetus to subsequent agricultural developments, these hostilities were allegedly detrimental to the export trades. After Norway, as part of the Danish Kingdom, came into the war on the French side in 1807, the market in England was barely accessible. And after the war, English duties in favor of Canadian timber presumably pro-

---

[14]See [G10], p. 26.

longed this situation until 1842. When, in 1814, the old union with
Denmark was dissolved, the recognized Danish market for Norwegian iron
was half lost.[15]

I will now argue that previous writers who talk about a prolonged
"post-Napoleonic depression" may have paid too much attention to institutional details and contemporary complaints. In any event, the empirical evidence we have regarding the developments of quantities of the
principal commodities exported does not bear out such bleak stories.[16]
It is true that exports of bar iron remained stagnant throughout the
period between 1815 and 1865. However, this export commodity was never
a really important part of the total compared to commodities such as
timber, fish products and shipping services. Exports of timber increased
from decade to decade. The average yearly rate of growth between 1816/25
and 1836-45 was 0.9 percent. This increase accelerates between 1836/45
and 1856/65 when the quantities exported of this commodity grew 2.7 percent per year.

The export trade in dried fish and salted herring developed happily during these fifty years with export volumes growing at yearly average rates of 2.6 percent and 2.0 percent respectively. In this particu-

---

[15]For more institutional details, consult Bull [B9], especially
pp. 262-63.

[16]The following relies on data on the quantities of the principal
Norwegian export commodities given in [G12], Tables 22 and 23, pp. 30-33.
It is perfectly clear that a fuller understanding of the impact of these
export developments would require price data as well as figures on quantities. Quite obviously, a substantial fall in export prices might mean
reduced values of exports despite increases in quantities. Such price
data is, to my knowledge, not available.

lar trade the most rapid growth took place during the first half of
the period.

Norwegian shipping had in the 18th century developed as a subsidiary to the timber trade, the ship owners often being the timber merchants
themselves. It experienced rapid development between 1800 and 1815, probably partly due to the Napoleonic wars, when the number of ships increased
from 1156 to 1673 and net tonnage grew at an average yearly rate of 0.8
percent. Some excess capacity probably developed and caused slower growth
during the following 20 years. The number of ships increased further to
2272 in 1835, but net tonnage remained fairly stagnant. It fell by about
35,000 net tons between a peak in 1815 and a trough in 1825, only to increase by almost 40,000 net tons during the following ten years. Some
falling off in gross investment in ships and boats for approximately 10
years following 1815 is therefore the main trust of the alleged post-
Napoleonic-war depression hypothesis.

An impressive expansion took place in shipping after 1825. Net
tonnage grew at an average yearly rate of 2.9 percent between 1825 and
1835, and during the following 30 years net tonnage increased almost
five-fold, or by 5.3 percent per year, while the number of ships more than
doubled. This rapid growth was facilitated by the liberalization and expansion of world trade. Norwegian ships began to carry goods between
foreign countries, at first Swedish timber to England in addition to domestic timber, and later all sorts of goods in all parts of the seven
seas. The sailing ships used were almost exclusively built in Norway.
Aside from the direct impact this must have had on Norwegian domestic in-

vestment, it must also have had some indirect or "backward linkage" effects through the use of Norwegian timber and ship-builders as inputs. By the end of the period reviewed Norway's merchant marine was the third largest in the world, with only Britain and the U.S.A. in front. One may conclude, then, that, although growth of exports was generally slower before 1835 than it was later on, a prolonged depression hypothesis regarding the early period is probably unwarranted.

What was the impact of these export developments on the growth of the aggregate Norwegian economy? To get a very crude indication of the possible magnitudes involved we can draw on value figures for the decade immediately following 1865. (All the figures referred to below are averages for the decade 1866-1875.) Exports of forestry and fishery products together with net shipping earnings made up over ninety percent of total exports of all goods and services. Together these three exports constituted almost one-fourth of Norwegian net domestic product in this time period. Net shipping earnings as a ratio of NNP amounted to more than 10 percent, and the respective ratios for forestry exports and fishing were 6.9 and 6.7 percent. Furthermore, investments in ships and boats made up more than one-fourth of gross fixed domestic capital formation or almost 4 percent of gross domestic product. Given these magnitudes during the decade immediately following 1865, it is probably fair to conclude that the rapid growth in the quantities exported that these three industries experienced before 1865 must have had a significant impact on the economy.[17]

---

[17]The separate importance of these three export trades in terms of their share of total employment is hard to assess. The census figures for 1865, which are not strictly comparable to subsequent census classifica-

After this brief review, what can we conclude about Norwegian economic development before 1865? It is probable that aggregate output rose after 1815 and significantly so after 1835. A more precise statement is probably unwarranted without considerable further research on the available primary statistical material. However, no major structural transformation of the economy took place in this period. On the eve of mass emigration, rural life still dominated and was characterized by labor intensive agriculture. Exports consisted of unprocessed raw materials, mostly timber and fishing products, in addition to shipping services. A small cotton industry and some engineering shops had been started during the 1840's and 1850's, but modern manufacturing industries were non-existent.

3.2. The Period 1865-1939

For this period we can draw on recently published research which carries the Norwegian national accounts back to 1865.[18]

3.2.1. Trends in the Growth of Aggregate Output, Capital and Labor.

Average annual growth rates for subperiods of the seventy-five years preceding World War II can be found in Table II-6. Growth rates of output and capital were calculated from constant 1938 price figures.

---

tions of employment by industry, are as follows: Agriculture and forestry 64.1 percent, navigation 4.7 percent, and fishery 4.9 percent. However, forestry, fishing and sailing were to a large extent employment of a seasonal nature which many workers, stating agriculture as their main occupation, had as subsidiary occupations. The 1865 census did not make adjustments for this fact.

[18]This work has been carried out by the Norwegian Central Bureau of Statistics. The major findings back to 1865 are reviewed in a recent publication authored by Bjerke [B6].

TABLE II-6

AVERAGE ANNUAL RATES OF GROWTH IN
PRODUCTION, REAL CAPITAL, LABOR FORCE, OUTPUT PER CAPITA,
OUTPUT PER MEMBER OF LABOR FORCE, FIXED REAL CAPITAL PER MEMBER OF
LABOR FORCE, AND THE GROWTH IN NET DOMESTIC PRODUCT BY "CAUSES"
Selected Periods 1865-1939*

	Time Periods	(1)**	(2)	(3)	(4)	(5)	(6)	(7)	(8)	(9)	(10)	(11)
(a)	1865-1874 to 1885-1894	1.7***	1.8	0.7	1.6	0.36	0.53	0.71	44.0	1.09	1.20	1.26
(b)	1885-1894 to 1910-1919	2.4	2.2	0.9	2.4	0.44	0.68	1.28	53.0	1.89	1.79	1.58
(c)	1910-1919 to 1930-1939	2.9	2.3	1.2	2.8	0.46	0.91	1.43	51.0	2.58	1.95	1.29
(d)	1865-1887	1.55	1.79	0.80	-	-	-	-	-	0.85	0.75	-
(e)	1887-1916	2.80	2.28	0.90	-	-	-	-	-	1.92	1.90	-
(f)	1916-1939	2.80	2.40	1.26	-	-	-	-	-	2.10	1.60	-

* Sources of Data: Columns (1) through (11), lines (a) through (c): [B6], Table 18,
p. 50 and Table 7, p. 32
Columns (1) and (9), lines (d) through (f) are computed from
[B1], Table 6, p. 56
Columns (2), (3) and (10), lines (d) through (f) computed from
[B6], Table 7, p. 32 and Table 12, p. 39.

** (1) Gross Domestic Product
(2) Fixed Real Capital Formation
(3) Labor Force
(4) Net Domestic Product
(5) Increases in NDP caused by increases in FRC
(6) Increases in NDP caused by increases in L
(7) Increases in NDP caused by residual factors
(8) Column (7) divided by Column (4) multiplied by 100
(9) GDP/P; or GDP per capita
(10) GDP/L; or GDP per member of L
(11) FRC/L; or FRC per member of L

*** All calculations are based on GDP and FRC in constant 1938 prices.

Gross Domestic Product increased almost six-fold between 1865 and 1939. The change in Net Domestic Product was of a similar magnitude. Before 1887 G.D.P. grew at an average annual rate of 1.55 percent. This yearly average increased to 2.80 percent after this date. Substantial gains were made in output per capita as well. The growth rates for the three sub-periods were 0.85, 1.92 and 2.10 percent respectively, causing this often-used index of economic well-being to stand at over three times its 1865 level in 1939.[19]

There is an apparent acceleration in the growth rate of both G.D.P. and G.D.P. per capita after 1887. This year marked the end of a ten-year-long depression during which aggregate output grew at only 0.3 percent per year and output per capita declined. However, the results of calculations of growth rates between single-year end points are sensitive to the selection of these points. The figures in lines a through c of Table II-6, which are yearly growth rates between ten-year averages, should be less biased in this respect.

Using the three sub-periods thus marked off, a picture of increase in the growth of G.D.P. and G.D.P. per capita from period to period emerges. However, the acceleration in economic growth starting around the 1890's still stands out. Between the first and the second period there

---

[19]If the level of output per capita in the United Kingdom (referring to the year 1938) is set equal to 100, the equivalent relative figure for Norway is found to be 89 in the same year. This is substantially below the U.S. figure of 143, but slightly above West-Germany at 84 and France at 75. These figures for 1938 were arrived at by the Central Bureau of Statistics of Norway, based on extrapolations of the study by Gilbert and Associates: Comparative National Products and Price Levels 1958). See [B1], Table 11, page 78.

was an increase in the growth of aggregate output of 0.7 percentage points.
This acceleration was even more marked in the growth of output per person
which changed from little over one percent to almost two percent per year.
These changes are accompanied by increases in rate of growth of capital
and labor inputs. The rate of growth of Fixed Real Capital and Labor
changed by 0.4 and 0.2 percentage points respectively. Thus the growth
of the fixed capital stock increased relatively more rapidly than the
stock of labor. Consequently the average yearly growth of real capital
per person of labor force stepped up markedly and grew even faster than
during the post-World War I period. Partially as a result of this, average labor productivity grew considerably faster after the 1890's than before this time.

How much of the growth in aggregate output was caused by inputs of
labor and capital as conventionally measured and how much was due to other
factors? Any detailed attention to this question is beyond the scope of
the present review. However, some results of previous research will be
briefly reported.[20] The figures in columns (5) through (8) of Table II-6
are based on estimates of an aggregate production function of the Cobb-
Douglas type where capital, labor, and technical progress enter symmetri-
cally and where the latter is assumed to grow at an exogenously given constant rate throughout the period. The elasticities of capital and labor
with respect to output were estimated to be 0.22 and 0.70 respectively,
indicating approximately constant returns with respect to these two fac-

---

[20]The following draws on Bjerke's work, see ibid., pages 48-52.

tors. Using these results we can split up the growth rate of Net Domestic Product according to the contributions made by the growth of capital, labor, and other factors along well-known lines.

During the three sub-periods marked off in Table II-6 the increases in the conventional inputs of fixed real capital and labor explain slightly less than half of the increase in Net Domestic Product, the rest being due to residual factors or technical progress very broadly defined. From column 8 we see that the _relative_ contribution of technical progress increased somewhat from 44 in the first sub-period to 53 during the period which saw an acceleration in the long-term rate of aggregate output growth. It remained above 50 during the third period.

There are several reasons, however, why this production-function approach is not likely to help us explain why the growth of the Norwegian economy accelerated after the 1890's. The first objection has to do with the nature of the aggregate production function that was employed. The figures in columns 5 through 8 are based on the estimated elasticities of a function in which technical progress is assumed to be "disembodied" or occurs independently of the advance in capital input as conventionally defined. The nature of the capital formation that took place in Norway starting in the late 1880's embodied considerable advances in technology, especially in the shipping and electrical-chemical industries, in the sense that they were based on radically new developments such as the switch from sail to steam ships. Some of these events will be reviewed in more detail below. These new investments were, in addition, to a considerable extent based on the availability of foreign financing. And that leads to the sec-

ond, and perhaps more fundamental, limitation of the production function
approach in this connection. It takes the rate of growth of capital
(and labor and technology for that matter) as exogenously given. Thus
the more fundamental question of what determines the rate of capital formation is left unanswered. To get a better understanding of why the
growth of the Norwegian economy accelerated after the 1890's one will
have to attempt to account for the causes of the observed acceleration
in the growth of capital formation and the other factors of production.

3.2.2. Long Swings in the Growth of Aggregate Output, Capital
and Labor. There are evidences of long swings in the development of the
Norwegian economy during this time period. The evidence regarding the
rate of growth of G.D.P., Fixed Real Capital, Labor Force and Labor Input
is set forth in Table II-7, panel A. From this table the impression
emerges that Norwegian economic development in these years was marked by
alternative periods of relatively rapid and slow economic growth. Furthermore, these periods lasted considerably longer than the ordinary
business cycle. The five periods of prosperity exhibiting an average
yearly rate of growth of G.D.P. of 2.9 percent per year or more lasted
on the average 7.4 years. For the years 1871-1916 the average period of
expansion equaled 10 years. The five stagnation periods marked off in
Table II-7 lasted on the average 7.4 years also, and, excluding the last
period, the average is 8 years. Measured from peak to peak, the average
duration of the long swing in the rate of growth of G.D.P. is 15.5 years
based on the entire 74-year period, and 18 years when the 1930's are
excluded. The trough to trough measures average 16 and 18.3 years respectively.

TABLE II-7

A. AVERAGE YEARLY RATES OF GROWTH OF GROSS AND NET DOMESTIC PRODUCT, FIXED REAL CAPITAL, LABOR FORCE AND LABOR INPUT IN NORWAY. Selected Periods 1865-1939. Percent per year.

(1) Time Periods	(2) GDP	(3) NDP	(4) FRC	(5) Labor Force	(6) Labor Input	(7) Labor Force Assuming No Emigration
1865-1871	1.6	1.4	1.6	0.9	0.8	1.9
1871-1877	3.6	3.6	2.3	1.4	1.8	1.8
1877-1887	0.3	0.2	1.6	0.3	0.2	1.7
1887-1899	2.9	2.9	2.1	0.9	1.0	1.6
1899-1905	0.4	0.2	1.7	0.5	0.3	1.8
1905-1916	4.0	4.0	2.8	1.0	1.1	1.6
1916-1926	1.4	1.3	2.2	1.2	0.7	
1926-1930	6.1	6.4	2.5	0.8	1.5	
1930-1935	1.5	1.4	1.6	1.5	0.9	
1935-1939	4.6	4.6	3.7	1.2	2.4	

B. PERIODS OF PROSPERITY AND STAGNATION IN THE ECONOMIC DEVELOPMENT OF THE UNITED STATES 1863-1914

(1) Periods of Prosperity	(2) Stagnation Periods
1863-1873	1873-1878
1878-1882	1882-1885
1885-1892	1892-1896
1896-1907	1907-1914

Sources of Data: Panel A. Columns (2) and (3): [B6], Table 11, p. 38
Column (4), same pub., Table 7, p. 32
Columns (5) and (6) computed by the author from unpublished data provided by Juul Bjerke.

Panel B. Taken from [G25].

Consider now how the long swings in Norwegian economic development compare with those marked off in the U.S. economy. Consult panels A and B of Table II-7. The impression of a considerable inversity in the pace of economic growth in the two economies before World War I emerges. The following years are characterized as periods of prosperity in the U.S. and as years of relatively slow growth in Norway: 1865-1871, 1878-1882, 1885-1887 and 1899-1905. Conversely, during these years the pace of Norwegian economic growth was relatively rapid while the U.S. economy experienced stagnation periods: 1873-1877, 1892-1896, and 1907-1914. Thus in 34 out of the 49 years between 1865 and 1914 one economy was growing slowly while the other was developing rapidly, and vice versa.

Consider now some of the possible reasons for the long swings in Norwegian economic growth. First, during the years of heavy Norwegian overseas emigration there were long swings in the rate of growth of the Norwegian labor force, as exhibited in Chart II-5. Consult also column (5) of Table II-7. As an approximation of the impact of overseas emigration on the rate of addition to the Norwegian economically active population, I computed what the rate of growth of the Norwegian labor force would have been assuming no overseas emigration between 1865 and 1916 ceteris paribus. During the entire period Norway "lost" more than 400,000 man-years through overseas emigration. Thus the average yearly growth of the Norwegian labor force during those 51 years was 0.8 percent while, assuming no other changes, with no emigration this rate would have been almost twice as high, or 1.5 percent per year.

The computations for the sub-periods between 1865 and 1916 are set

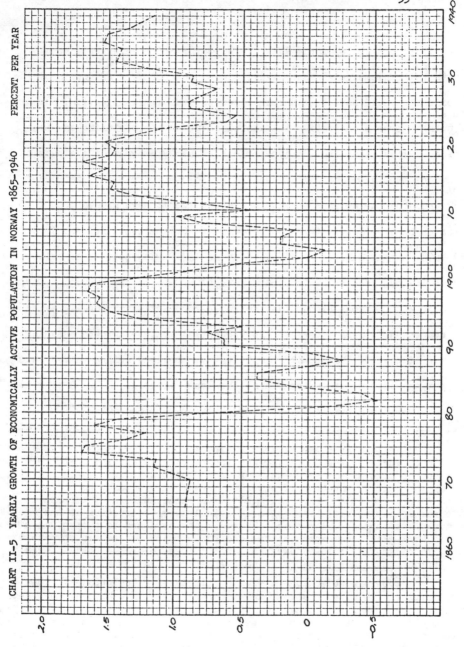

CHART II-5 YEARLY GROWTH OF ECONOMICALLY ACTIVE POPULATION IN NORWAY 1865-1940

PERCENT PER YEAR

55

forth in column (7) of Table II-7.[21] A picture of a relatively steady growth pattern emerges. Each figure shows what the rate of growth of the labor force would have been during a sub-period of no emigration, but allowing overseas emigration to take place up to the beginning of each period. It is clear that during periods of heavy emigration the rate of growth of the labor force is reduced many-fold. For example, between 1877 and 1887 the average yearly growth rate would have been almost 6 times as high, or 1.7 percent as compared to 0.3 percent; between 1899 and 1905, almost 4 times as high. Conversely, during periods of relatively low overseas emigration, the rate of growth of the Norwegian labor force is 2 to 3 times higher than during periods of heavy out-migration and consequently much closer to the "potential" rate of growth assuming no emigration. One may conclude, then, that the long swings in overseas emigration was a major factor behind the long swings in the rate of growth of the Norwegian labor force, at least between 1865 and 1916.[22]

---

[21]I arrived at these figures as follows: We have data on the actual labor force at the beginning and end of each sub-period and the absolute number of overseas emigrants for each year classified by age and sex. I took the absolute numbers of male and female emigrants between 15 and 59 years of age for each period and multiplied these numbers by the respective participation rates for males and females, thus arriving at the "loss" in man-years through emigration. By adding this "loss" to the actual size of the Norwegian labor force at the end of each period, we can compute wh. the rate of growth of the Norwegian labor force would have been in each sub-period, ceteris paribus, with no overseas emigration at all.

[22]A possible objection to such hypothetical calculations is that, for example, with no emigration, unemployment might have been higher, natural increase lower, etc., than it actually was. On second thought, this is not so clear because, as we shall see in a moment, the emigration response itself may have caused for example the demand for (urban) construction to have been lower than it would have been with no emigration. And the labor force is determined by prior births and survival rates. At any rate, I contend that the ceteris paribus assumption is not so strong as to alter the basic conclusion drawn from the calculations made.

Consider, secondly, the rate of development of gross fixed capital

formation in Norway before 1916 as exhibited in Chart II-6. It will be

seen that there are long swings in the level of Total Gross Fixed Capital

Formation which are in almost perfect conformity with the swings in the

rate of growth of Gross Domestic Product. And since the Norwegian invest-

ment series in Chart II-6 refer to yearly unsmoothed figures, it cannot

be said that these long swings are created by the artificial smoothing of

yearly numbers. Furthermore, the swings in Total Gross Fixed Investment

are a reflection of the marked long swings in two of its major sub-compo-

nents, namely, Gross Fixed Capital Formation in Buildings and Other Con-

structions, and Other Transportation Equipment , Machinery, Implements, etc.

respectively. See the lower half of Chart II-6. These two sub-components

made up roughly three-fourths of Total Gross Investment in Norway during

the period before 1916, while Gross Investment in Buildings and other con-

structions alone accounted for almost 50 percent of Total Gross Fixed Capi-

tal Formation during the same period.[23] One may hypothesize that the

volume of house-building largely determines the level of certain other

forms of investment, such as the construction of urban public utilities,

and it is known to have a significant effect on the demand for consumers'

durables in the form of, for example, fittings and furnishings.

---

[23]The third major component of Total Norwegian Gross Fixed Capital
Formation before 1916 was Gross Investments in Ships and Boats accounting
for roughly one-fifth or 20 percent of the total. This gross investment
series does not exhibit long swings but rather fluctuations in its level
that resembles the shorter business cycle, and its peaks and troughs conforms very closely with the cycles in Net National Income in the United
Kingdom. Compare the figures in [B6], Table XV, p. 134, and Table B, pp.
150-51, with for example Matthews [B52], diagram 9, p. 217.

CHART II-6   GROSS NEW CONSTRUCTION IN U.S.A. (1) 5 Year Moving Average. 1929 prices.
TOTAL GROSS FIXED CAPITAL FORMATION (2), GROSS FIXED CAPITAL FORMATION IN BUILDINGS + OTHER CONSTRUCTION (3),
AND GROSS FIXED CAPITAL FORMATION IN OTHER TRANSPORTATION EQUIPMENT, MACHINERY, IMPLEMENTS (4) IN NORWAY
Yearly Series in 1910 prices.

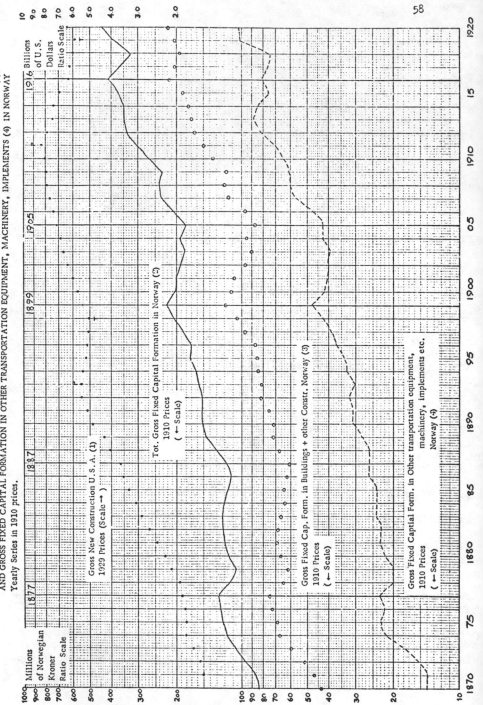

However, it is the peculiarity of its behavior rather than merely
its quantitative importance that makes house-building require separate
discussion in an account of long swings since there is suggestive evidence of close causal connections between population swings and the well-
known 20-year cycle in investments in buildings and other construction.
Its waves were doubtless influenced by many factors: by income change
itself and finance, by speculation and by the under- and over-shooting
inherent in any lagged capital-stock adjustment process. Accepting all
that, however, Burnham Campbell has shown that by far the bulk of variation in house building in the U.S. was associated with population change
weighted by what he calls headship rates, that is, by the propensity of
people in different age groups to form independent households. See Campbell [A8] and [B10]. For evidence relating to Great Britain, consult
Lewis [B48]. The long swings in the rate of growth of the Norwegian population between the ages of 20 and 39 was described in some detail in section 2.3 above. There it was shown that prior birth and contemporary
emigration swings caused these swings in the rate of growth of age-groups
in which headship rates were high. It may therefore be hypothesized that
it was the wave of emigration which, along with the echo-effects of prior
births, was a dominant influence on Norwegian house building during this
time period. During these same years in Norway there was a very pronounced inverse relation between the rate of overseas emigration and the
rate of townward migration within Norway. (For further evidence and discussion on this point, the reader is referred to Chapter IV below.) Since
townward migration was an important source of building demand, a high rate

of emigration thus served to discourage building by more than the absolute number of those migrating might suggest.

Having said so much, some of the possible causes of the long swings in the Norwegian economic growth and its apparent inverse relationship with the pace of U.S. economic development can now be briefly restated. It was founded chiefly, but not entirely, on the emigration response itself.[24] Long swings in overseas emigration to the U.S. drew off workers who were potential migrants to Norwegian cities and thus caused long swings in the growth of the Norwegian (industrial) labor supply. It was, furthermore, a major explanatory factor behind the long swings in the level of investment in Norwegian (urban) building and construction.[25] The American booms probably competed for European (British) capital in addition to labor. Compare for example the inverse relationship between construction investment in the United States and Norway exhibited in Chart II-6. Foreign investment in Norway became an important factor in the 1890's, and during the period up to World War I it conformed closely to the long swings in economic growth. Thus rapid economic growth in the United States may have cut short the availability of foreign capital for Norwegian investment projects, depressing the rate of Norwegian domestic capital formation, ceteris paribus.

---

[24]For an analysis of the causes of this response, see the econometric model of Norwegian labor emigration to the United States developed and tested in Chapter V below.

[25]In a recent theoretical paper, J. P. Lewis has shown, employing a simple two-country model, that in the absence of shocks inverse long cycles in output are likely to appear through the housing sector alone, if emigration is allowed, and if there is a basic population cycle. Consult [A26].

To be sure, these statements are more in the nature of suggestive hypotheses than rigorously proven relationships. And certain important aspects of the growth of aggregate demand have not been discussed. I am thinking especially of Norwegian export developments during this period since it may be assumed that aggregate consumption adjusts passively to income changes along well-known lines. For example, the retardation or decline of British home investment, which moved inversely with domestic investment in the U.S., may very well have affected Britain's demand for Norwegian exports. At any rate, there is a suggestion that this slowed down industrial growth elsewhere in Scandinavia.[26]

A more rigorous and complete study of the growth of the Norwegian economy during this period ideally requires a full-fledged macro-economic-demographic model in which the above hypothesized relationships would be a part. This is beyond the scope of the present study and will have to await further research on historical economic growth in Norway.

3.2.3. The Structural Transformation of the Norwegian Economy. Before 1930 estimates of Gross Domestic Product by separate industries are available only for the single year 1910. Fairly reliable disaggregated labor force data exist at each census date back to 1875. To get an estimate of the distribution of output by industry at this early date, the observed average labor productivity in each industry for the year 1910 was multiplied by the available labor force data for 1875. Thus the rela-

---

[26]For the relation between Britain and America, the standard source is Brinley Thomas [B67]. See also Wilkinson's study of Swedish economic growth [A43].

tive output figures for 1875 are, at best, crude indicators of orders of magnitude.[27]

Table II-8 provides clear evidence of the rapid structural transformation that the Norwegian economy underwent between 1875 and 1939. The share of primary production in total output fell from over one-third to slightly over ten percent in sixty-five years. In terms of labor force, agriculture and forestry alone employed almost half of this total at the beginning of the period. This share was almost halved by 1930. Corresponding increases took place in the remaining four groups, most of it occurring in the second one consisting of mining, manufacturing, construction, gas and water.

The growth of agriculture after 1865 stands in sharp contrast to developments earlier in the nineteenth century. Most Norwegian agriculture was particularly ill-equipped to meet the increasing foreign competition, especially in grain production, that resulted from the opening up of new territories abroad and the reduction in transportation costs in the latter half of the nineteenth century. Between 1875 and 1910 the economically active population in agriculture (and forestry) actually decreased by more than ten percent and was still below its absolute 1875 level in 1930. Similarly, the area of cultivated farmland in grain and potato production was considerably smaller in 1910 than in 1865. These

---

[27]It is very probable that average labor productivity in agriculture grew considerably slower than in for example manufacturing. Thus a calculation applying 1910 industry productivity figures to a much earlier year will obviously yield biased estimates of the respective shares at the early date. Looking at the changes in relative shares of aggregate output between 1875 and 1910 as exhibited in Table II-8, it is very likely that the transformation out of primary industries and into mining, manufacturing and construction as recorded there is underestimated.

TABLE II-8

G.D.P. AND LABOR FORCE DISTRIBUTED BY INDUSTRY
(Percent distributions at selected census dates)*

A. GDP (At Current Prices By Industry)	1875	1890	1910	1930	1939
(1) Agriculture, forestry, fishing, whaling	35.4	-	23.7	16.7	11.5
(2) Mining, manufacturing, construction, gas and water	21.8	-	26.2	30.3	33.6
(3) Transport and communication	13.6	--	11.3	12.6	15.4
(4) Trade, banking, and insurance	10.1	-	17.8	17.0	18.5
(5) Other private and public services; of which services from dwellings and domestic services	19.1	-	21.0 / 9.2 / 4.4	23.4 / 10.3 / 2.2	20.9 / 8.5 / 1.7
TOTAL GDP = Col. 1+2+3+4+5	100.0	-	100.0	100.0	100.0

B. Labor Force By Industry					
(1a) Agriculture and forestry	47.3	42.1	33.5	28.9	-
(1b) Fishing, whaling and sealing	4.6	7.1	5.5	7.0	
(1) = 1a+1b	51.9	49.2	39.0	35.9	
(2) Mining, manufacturing, construction, gas and water	18.1	21.9	25.0	26.5	-
(3) Transport and communications	7.7	7.2	7.4	8.3	-
(4) Trade, banking, and insurance	3.5	5.0	7.1	10.5	-
(5) Other private and public services	14.2	15.3	17.8	18.6	
(6) Industry unknown	4.7	1.4	3.7	0.3	
TOTAL LABOR FORCE = Col. 1+2+3+4+5+6	100.0	100.0	100.0	100.0	

* Sources of data: Panel A: [B6], Table 20, p. 53
  Panel B: [B6], Table 21, p. 54 and
  [A23], Table 4, p. 15.

reductions in the inputs of labor and land were accompanied by adoption of mechanized methods. In 1875 only 1,299 mowers and reapers were in use, while this number increased to 31,552 in 1900 and reached 56,310 by 1910, a fifty-fold increase in thirty-five years. Thus in 1910 approximately every fifth farm unit had a mower or reaper. However, most of the farms were still extremely small, especially by U.S. standards. An agricultural census taken in 1907 showed that over one-third of the farm units were of the size of approximately one acre or less, and more than two-thirds of all farms had less than five acres of cultivated land. Only seven percent of the farm units employed more than twenty-five acres. Furthermore, little or no tariff protection was offered the farm sector as a compensation for the almost continual fall in domestic prices caused by the foreign competition.[28] It was probably the larger farmers who were able to sruvive the transformation towards production mainly for the market by adopting more capital-intensive techniques. But for the small farmer or cotter limited by a tiny plot of land and little or no capital, these must have been difficult years indeed. By the first decade of the twentieth century Norway had to import seventy percent of total consumption of grain, and only forty percent of the total use of potatoes was produced domestically.

Industrialization, on the other hand, proceeded relatively rapidly after 1865. The total economically active population in mining, manufacturing and construction more than doubled between 1875 and 1920, and most

[28]For a detailed account of the developments of tariffs in the 19th century, see Lieberman [B49].

of this increase took place during the last decade of the nineteenth century and the second decade of the twentieth during which the labor force
in these industries grew at an average yearly rate of between three and
four percent. Between 1900 and 1910 and 1920 and 1930 the absolute size
of the industrial labor force actually decreased. The industrialization
process was based largely on the development of the traditional export industries, producing for the rapidly growing world market. However, considerable transformation took place within these industries after 1865.

The saw and planning mills, whose exports of wood in a very slightly
refined shape had expanded considerably before 1865, reached their peak
as early as the first half of the 1870's. However, new inventions that
made possible the use of mechanical and, later, chemical pulp for the manu-
facture of paper presented new openings to Norwegian industry. This development meant adoption of new, more capital-intensive technology, larger
firms, and a need for new labor skills. In 1875, no enterprise in the
pulp and paper industry had more than two hundred workers. In 1909, there
were fifteen such enterprises. By 1914 the export value of this new industry was more than twice as large as that from the saw and planning mills.
A considerable part of the capital for the largest and most efficient enterprises were foreign. In 1909, more than one-third of the whole capital in
the pulp and paper industry was owned by foreigners.[29]

Foreign capital was also active in the development of an electro-
chemical industry, based on innovations in the technology of hydro-elec-

[29]For more details on the industrialization process, especially before 1914, the reader is referred to the paper by Bull [B9]. The role of
foreign investments in Norwegian economic development is analyzed by Stonehill [B65].

tricity, and mining. The transformation of these industries was paralleled by the industrialization of shipping. This particular industry experienced structural difficulties after the boom of the 1870's which marked the end of the glorious era of sail. The steamer, with vastly superior cargo-carrying capacity and reduced crew requirements per net ton, had already been adopted extensively in other leading seafaring nations by this time period. In Norway such a transformation was delayed by the very wide dispersion of sailing ships among a host of small ship-owners. Many of these shippers lacked the capacity, notably in the form of capital, to make the switch. In the 1880's, however, the steamer fleet began seriously to expand. In 1914 the steamer tonnage was more than double that of the sailing ships, and after World War I the sailing vessels quickly disappeared.

All of the industries most heavily involved in the industrialization process produced mainly for foreign markets. Thus the transformation of the Norwegian economy, briefly sketched above, was to a considerable extent due to the ability of these industries to capitalize on the opening up of the world economy and the rapid growth of world trade, especially before 1914. The relative share of total exports of goods and services in G.D.P. (both measured in current prices) stood above thirty percent on the average between 1865 and 1939. Gross freight shipping earnings accounted for an average of thirty-nine percent of total exports of goods and services; timber, wood pulp, paper and paper products made up roughly twenty percent; and the relative share of mining, metals, chemical products and other industrial products averaged over seventeen percent. Together these three groups accounted for over three-fourths of total exports between 1865 and 1939. Thus, the transformation and development of the Norwegian economy up to 1939 seems in many respects a textbook example of the virtues of international division of labor and "export-led growth." As a result of all these developments, the level of income per capita in Norway was comparable to or above that of the other developed countries in Western Europe on the eve of World War II.

II-4. Possible Economic Causes of the Secular Fall in Deaths and Births

The so-called laws of "stages" in population growth invariably state that growth is initiated by a fall in the death rate. This upsets the "old balance" of high birth and death rates, causing increase to accelerate. The demographic transition is completed when, with a delay of unspecified length, the birth rate is reduced also so that a "new balance" is achieved.[30] According to a recent statement, the sustained acceleration in natural increase, caused by the initial fall in the death rate, will in turn set in motion a "multi-phasic response" of which the eventual fall in the birth rate is one.[31] Now, it is clear that such

---

[30] On "stage" theories of population growth, see for example Blacker [A7]. A more detailed review of this literature can be found in Thomlinson [B72], especially pages 18-25.

[31] "Although generally overlooked because of our preoccupation with the contraceptive issue, the fact is that every country in northwest Europe reacted to its persistent excess of births over deaths with virtually the entire range of possible responses. Regardless of nationality, language, and religion, each industrializing nation tended to postpone marriage, to increase celibacy, to resort to abortion, to practice contraception in some form, and to emigrate overseas". Davis [A10], pages 350-351.

statements are good historical descriptions of much of recorded population growth in the nineteenth and twentieth centuries. In particular,
as was briefly documented in Section II-2 above, the two hundred years
of population growth in Norway between 1741 and 1940 could for descriptive purposes be roughly divided into four "stages" or periods.

During the eighteenth century the "old balance" prevailed with
high birth and death rates resulting in an average yearly rate of population growth around 0.5 percent.[32] In the course of the second "stage",
spanning the sixty years between the long swing troughs of 1809 and 1869,
the natural rate of increase more than doubled largely as a result of a
rapidly falling death rate. The rest of the century comprises the third
"stage." Natural increase stabilized at a record level of between 1.3
and 1.4 percent per annum. However, the emigration "response" reduced
domestic population growth to half this rate. Finally, the "demographic
revolution" was completed during the fourth "stage" in the twentieth century as the birth "response" reduced natural increase to its eighteenth
century level despite continually falling death rates.

The difficulty with such a stage framework, as with similar ones
constructed to account for "stages" in economic growth, is that, at best,
it isolates periods of marked changes. Generally, such theories encounter

---

[32]Birth and death rates were high relative to what they became in
subsequent periods, and they corresponded well to the Scandinavian averages in the eighteenth century. However, as Gille pointed out, the average Scandinavian crude birth and death rates before the Napoleonic wars
were lower than those in England during most of the nineteenth century and
in Germany during the whole of that century. Furthermore, they stood below average birth and death rates recorded in such diverse countries as
for example the U.S.S.R., Egypt, Israel and Chile in the late 1940's. Consult [A15], p. 30.

difficulties in explaining why the changes took place and why they took place at different times in different regions or nations. From our point of view we are merely interested in finding out to what extent some of the _marked_ secular changes that took place in Norwegian population growth were the _result_ of economic developments or, alternatively, sprang from forces which were, from an economic point of view, fortuitous. In the following we shall, if only in a preliminary way, ask ourselves this question with respect to the marked pre-industrial decline in mortality. Then we turn very briefly to the fall in fertility that set in as Norway became an increasingly industrialized country.

4.1. Economic Developments and the Pre-Industrial Fall in Deaths

The acceleration in population growth in Norway was mainly due to a reduced mortality pattern. Perhaps the most striking change was the disappearance of the so-called "dismal peaks" in the death rate. Thus on the surface it seems that, to use Malthusian terminology, the positive checks to population growth ceased to operate, at least in its extreme form.[33] Can we trace this change to economic events? Clearly we have to

---

[33]Curiously enough, Malthus himself seemed to think that the preventive check was the prevalent one in pre-industrial Norway. He traveled to Norway in 1799, and in a chapter in his famous Essay entitled _Of the checks to population in Norway_ he writes: "...we must feel assured, that as the positive checks have been so small, the preventive checks must have been proportionally great...." (Quote taken from [B14], p. 34.) Referring to the discussion in section 2.2.2 of this chapter, we can only agree with Drake who concludes: "That Malthus failed to see the important role of the positive check in Norway's demographic history is doubly ironical. First, because it was a fall in mortality which propelled Norway into half a century of very rapid population growth after 1815. Second, and perhaps more important, because it exposed the weakness of his research method," op. cit., p. 38.

argue in terms of an agricultural revolution rather than an industrial one since, as was briefly alluded to above, industrialization took hold at a much later date in Norway.

In order to pursue such a hypothesis, if only in a very preliminary fashion, consider the following simple relationships. Assume, first, that we can ignore births so that changes in population stem largely from changes in deaths. Changes in deaths, in turn, are hypothesized to be a function of two sets of factors: autonomous factors like the stock and application of medical knowledge on the one hand, and the level of income per capita on the other. Larger incomes per head means for instance a higher level of consumption including a more adequate diet, better housing and clothing, etc. Thus we have

$$(4.1.1) \quad \frac{dP}{P} = \frac{dD}{D} = e\left(\frac{O}{P} ; M\right) \quad \text{where}$$

where P = population, D = deaths, O = aggregate output, and
M = exogenous medical factors.

Suppose, further, that aggregate output or income is a function of the inputs of labor and land and the level of technology according to the following conventional production function

$$(4.1.2) \quad O = f(A ; L ; P)$$

where A = an index of productivity and L = land. For simplicity I
do not differentiate between population and labor input.

Assume that in such a pre-industrial economy Say's law operates so that the main problem is simply whether the aggregate supply of goods and services per capita will increase.

Consider now the hypothetical case in which the above macro production function is of the Cobb-Douglas type and linearly homogeneous amounting to the economic assumption of constant returns to scale. We can then specify (4.1.2) as follows:

$$(4.1.3) \quad O = AL^{\alpha}P^{1-\alpha} = A\left(\frac{L}{P}\right)^{\alpha} \cdot P.$$

Thus

$$(4.1.4) \quad \frac{O}{P} = A\left(\frac{L}{P}\right)^{\alpha}$$

and

$$(4.1.5) \quad \frac{\partial O}{\partial P} = AL^{\alpha} (1-\alpha) P^{-\alpha} = A (1-\alpha) \left(\frac{L}{P}\right)^{\alpha}.$$

This brings out the well-known properties that, regarding for the moment A as a positive constant, both $\frac{O}{P}$ and $\frac{\partial O}{\partial P}$ are functions of the $\frac{L}{P}$ ratio. In other words, as long as the land-polulation ratio is kept constant (whatever the absolute levels of L and P), average output per capita will be constant, too. Thus equal proportionate changes in L and P will leave output per head unchanged. Therefore, dY/Y is greater than dP/P at a given level of per capita output or income if the rate of land increase exceeds the rate of population increase at that level of output per head. Otherwise, under these conditions, and assuming no change in M, sustained increases in dP/P will not occur.

To break out of such a "Malthusian" or "low-level equilibrium" con-

dition, then, one or several of the following must occur. One possibility is a sustained increase in the land-population ratio. Alternatively
application of a major innovation or continually improving production
techniques may lead to increases in output per head; i.e., technological
improvements leads to upward "shifts" in A. Finally, changes in M may
occur independently of economic events. Given the above assumptions,
however, the latter event must be accompanied by one of the other two.
Otherwise the resulting rapid population growth will soon reduce output
per head and thus, in turn, lead to a reduction in population growth.

Is there any empirical evidence of any such changes in Norway
after the Napoleonic wars? As was mentioned in section 3.1 above, we
cannot establish in any rigorous way that income per capita increased
significantly before 1865. But som indirect evidence bearing on this
question was presented. For example, the area of cultivated land increased at the average yearly rate of 1.2 percent between 1820 and 1835
and 1.4 percent during the following 30 years, while the domestic Norwegian population grew 1.0 percent per year during the same two periods.
If we are willing to use the rural population between 20 and 60 years of
age as a crude proxy for potential agricultural labor force, the land-
labor ratio increased by about 20 percent between 1825 and 1865. Furthermore, recall that there were other additions to the stock of agricultural capital in the form of new and improved machinery and implements.

That leads us to the second factor, namely, improved (agricultural) technology. The productivity increases in Norwegian agriculture

and some of their possible sources were reviewed in some detail above
and will not be repeated here. Another innovation, such as the introduction of the potato, must have been of importance also. The potato proved
itself a more reliable crop than grain and one that could be grown on
land that would support little else. Thus the introduction of this new
major crop may not only have increased the land area that could be prof-
itably cultivated, it may also have reduced the year to year fluctuations
in the food supply.

Such developments are consistent with possible sustained increases
in output per head which, in the simple framework set forth above, allows
an increase in the rate of growth of population via a reduction in deaths.
However, it is quite clear that such evidence is short of establishing
in a more rigorous way that Norway escaped from a "low-level equilibrium"
trap during this period. What we can say is that the domestic supply of
food per capita must have improved considerably compared to the eighteenth
century. Recall that recorded gross domestic agricultural output per
capita tripled between the first decade of the nineteenth century and
1865. In addition, the expanding export trades must have facilitated regular importation of grain. Both these economic developments are consistent with a reduced mortality pattern.

The more conventional Malthusian model, where the link between
economic factors and mortality is largely through the adequacy of the food
supply rather than income per capita, has been under attack in recent work
in Scandinavian economic history. In a detailed study of Swedish mortality patterns, Utterström stressed the importance of the third factor men-

tioned above, namely such non-economic factors as epidemics and disease. See [A39].[34] He argued that not only did harvest failures reflect weather and not population pressure, the variations and severity of disease were due primarily to climactic changes. This argument was applied with special force to infant mortality. It is clear that Norway, to approximately the same extent as Sweden, lies in great part in the climactic margin for grain cultivation. And although all the major peaks in the deaths, notably the ones in 1741-1742, 1748, 1773 and 1809, occurred in years when the grain harvests failed, one may argue that bad weather to some extent caused these. However, in the Norwegian case this is not the whole story. Another necessary condition for disasters to happen would be that imports of grain from abroad were largely insufficient. For example, in 1809, when both exports and imports were greatly hampered by the Napoleonic war, grain prices in Bergen rose seven-fold and the food shortage was reportedly acute.

Vaccination against smallpox was carried out on an increasing scale throughout the first half of the nineteenth century, still only a very small proportion of the Norwegian population became protected by it. It is highly unlikely that smallpox accounted for a greater proportion of deaths in Norway than in Sweden, yet in no decade during the period 1751-1800 were more than sixteen percent of deaths amongst Swedes over the age of one year attributed to it.[35] So even if deaths from smallpox fell

---

[34]Utterström's criticism was directed mainly against Heckscher's Malthusian interpretation of Swedish population developments as expounded, for example, in [A19].

[35]Utterström [A39], pp. 162-65.

markedly after 1815, this medical factor is far from sufficient to explain

the marked change in the character of the Norwegian death rate after 1815.

None of these factors are mutually exclusive. Improved agricul-

tural technology will make production more resistant to the vagaries of

the weather, a more adequate diet will increase resistance to disease, etc.

However, given the present amount of evidence, one might conclude that

economic developments must have been a necessary, if not sufficient, con-

dition for the acceleration in population growth after 1809. A more de-

tailed specification of the exact mechanism at work is a topic for con-

tinued research in Norwegian economic history.

4.2. Economic Developments and the Fall in Births

Demographers and sociologists have devoted a large share of their

research time to find an explanation of the secular decline in fertility

that has occurred in most developed countries. A host of ideas and specu-

lations suggested by such terms as urbanization, industrialization, social

mobility, the changed status of women, decline in religious interest, etc.,

have been advanced.[36] Some of these factors, perhaps most of them, are

---

[36]The enormous demographic literature on this topic was summarized
in a fairly recent report by the United Nations thus: "Whereas certain
writers have held that modern life has tended to reduce reproductive capacity, most recent writers have emphasized that the decline in family
size has been brought about by the practice of family limitation. Related
to this attitude towards family limitation are a complex of inter-related
economic and social factors, such as the shift of the population from
country to city, the desire to improve one's own social and economic position or that of one's children, the changes in the status and role of
women in society, the improvement of the level of living, the increasing
expenses of rearing children, a decline in religious interest and a decline in mortality" [G24], p. 96.

related to both the process of industrialization and the decline in fertility, but how? Recently, more specific economic explanations of fertility have emerged. These assume that motivations with respect to family
size are basically rational and based to a large extent on economic considerations so that the demand for children will, like any other economic
good, be determined by benefits and costs broadly interpreted.

Leibenstein distinguished among three types of utility to be derived from an additional birth and two types of cost. A child may provide
"psychic pleasure" in the form of consumption and protect against the in-
security of old age. The child may also, as a productive agent, contribute to family income. Costs consist at the expenditures on a child until
it is self-supporting and in addition opportunities lost due to an additional child like for example inability of mothers to work. [B47], pages
161-62. It is then hypothesized that the utilities connected with the
provision of security and the child as a productive agent will decline
with increases in per capita income. On the other hand, the costs of
rearing children will assertedly rise rapidly as the economy becomes increasingly industrialized. The utility and cost functions involved, Leibenstein theorizes, are shaped such that beyond a certain "threshold" rate
of change of income per capita, all these factors will cause a reduction
in fertility.

Becker considers his model a "generalization and development" of
the Malthusian model [B4], page 209. The main difference from the original Malthusian setting is that the growth of knowledge about contraception
allows each family to have almost perfect control over both the number and

spacing of its births. Thus the decision of how many children to have
can be analyzed within the conventional framework of consumer theory since
children can be considered as a durable consumer good. Furthermore,
Becker argues that a family must determine not only how many children it
shall have but also the amount spent on them. The more expensive children are "higher quality" children. He speculates that the income effect
is positive for both the quantity and quality of children, but that the
quantity elasticity should be small compared to the quality elasticity.
If this is correct, the demand for children should, ceteris paribus, increase with increases in per capita income. On the surface, then, Becker's
model seems to contradict the Leibenstein model on this point.

As an instrument of historical interpretation, the chief point about
Becker's theory is that he assumes that in the early 19th century, the
actual family size was larger than the desired size, but spread of contraception made it possible to reduce this gap. So birth rates fell historically even though, in equilibrium, they would tend to rise with income.
Leibenstein, on the other hand, does not seem to assume that there was an
initial disequilibrium. He hypothesizes that, as income per capita increases beyond a certain point, quality expenditures per child increase to
such an extent that parents tend to reduce their demand for children.

Both arguments are a priori plausible, and the question can only
be settled on empirical grounds. Unfortunately, empirical studies on how
the various benefits and costs have actually behaved since the onset of
the fertility decline in developed countries are, to my knowledge, largely
non-existent. Rigorous tests of these alternative economic theories on

the micro-level will therefore have to await the availability of pertinent survey data. In the following I will therefore limit myself to a
preliminary look at the observed reduction in aggregate births in Norway
in the early 20th century.

There are, of course, no unique criteria that would enable us to
date exactly when the sustained decline in the Norwegian birth rate set
in. Examination of early data, however, indicates that the marked
changes started around the turn of the 20th century. Consequently, the
following trend relations, estimated by the classical least squares
method, were applied to the period 1901-1931.

(4.2.1)   TB = 65650 - 15.62 t^2 , $\bar{R}^2$ = 0.6697
                    (1.986)   D.W = 0.6093

(4.2.1)   UB = 20150 - 11.65 t^2 , $\bar{R}^2$ = 0.6761
                    (1.461)   D.W = 1.7826

(4.2.3)   RB = 45500 - 3.962t^2 , $\bar{R}^2$ = 0.0890
                    (1.998)   D.W = 0.9397

(4.2.4)   TGFR = 0.3218 - 0.00014 t^2 , $\bar{R}^2$ = 0.9411
                    (0.0000066) D.W = 0.9925

(4.2.5)   UGFR = 0.3041 - 0.00021 t^2 , $\bar{R}^2$ = 0.7989
                    (0.0000019) D.W = 1.7448

(4.2.6)   RGFR = 0.3306 - 0.00012 t^2 , $\bar{R}^2$ = 0.8252
                    (0.0000097) D.W = 1.3461

where TB = the total absolute number of births
      UB = the absolute number of urban births
      RB = the absolute number of rural births

TGFR = the total general fertility rate[37]

UGFR = the urban general fertility rate

RGFR = the rural general fertility rate

t = time in years

$\bar{R}^2$ = the coefficient of multiple determination corrected
for degrees of freedom

D.W = the Durbin-Watson statistic.

The numbers in parentheses below the estimated regression coefficients refer to the estimated standard errors of these coefficients.

The fits of equations (4.2.1) through (4.2.6) are quite good as judged by the estimated coefficients of multiple determination corrected for degrees of freedom. And as far as equations (4.2.2), (4.2.5) and (4.2.6) are concerned, one can reject the hypothesis of serial correlation in the estimated residuals at the .02 level of probability, indicating correct specification of these "birth transition" relationships. We have, furthermore, that $\frac{dUGFR}{dt} = -0.00042\ t$ and $\frac{dRGFR}{dt} = 0.00024\ t$. This shows how these general fertility rates declined with respect to time between 1901 and 1931. Thus, aggregate urban fertility declined almost twice as fast as aggregate rural fertility.

Having said so much, however, it is clear that time itself does not explain anything. In this case it is just a dummy variable for the real causal factors involved. One such factor, namely income per capita, was

---

[37]The general fertility figures refer to the absolute number of births divided by the absolute number of married females between 20 and 45 years of age each year. The resulting figures were not multiplied by a constant, e.g., 1000, which is sometimes done.

suggested by the discussion above. It is, furthermore, possible that
reduction in infant mortality might conceivably influence the number of
births. That is, if a certain number of children is desired by a family,
fewer births are needed to produce this desired number as infant mortality declines. The following relationships were therefore estimated for
the same time period.

$$(4.2.7) \quad TB = 88070 - 42.78 \; GDP/P \; , \quad \bar{R}^2 = 0.6290$$
$$(5.94) \quad\quad D.W = 0.5861$$

$$(4.2.8) \quad TB = 36900 + 359.50 \; IM \quad , \quad \bar{R}^2 = 0.4966$$
$$(64.99) \quad\quad D.W. = 0.5342$$

where GDP/P = a five-year moving average of Gross Domestic
Product per capita during the five years prior
to the year of birth, and

IM = the infant mortality rate in the year prior
to the year of births.

These results indicate that statistically significant relationships exist between births and both income per capita and infant mortality
on the macro level. The regression coefficient of births with respect to
infant mortality has the expected sign, and the estimated birth-income
relationship is negative. However, the estimated Durbin-Watson statistic
indicates that both relationships are underspecified.[38] As models of the
birth transition in Norway these relationships are, at best, incomplete.

---

[38]Attempts to include both GDP/P and IM as explanatory variables
in the same equation were unsuccessful largely because these two variables are highly multicollinear with a zero-order correlation coefficient
of - 0.878. As they stand, then, the regression coefficients estimated
by ordinary least squares in (4.2.7) and (4.2.8) are inefficient ones. In
further work one should probably apply generalized least squares.

More importantly, perhaps, if one attempts to use for example equation (4.2.7) to predict births after 1930, the model would do badly. It would predict a continued fall in births as income per capita rose steadily beyond the 1930's. However, as is well known, the Norwegian birth rate rebounded after World War II to an average level which is intermediate between that found during World War I and the trough level in the 1930's. In other words, the relationship between income per capita and births in the immediate post-World War II period was seemingly positive, not negative.

Several interpretations of this last phenomenon is possible. One would be that the basic long run relationship between these two aggregates is an inverse one, and that the post-World War II baby-boom was an abnormal deviation from a downward trend caused by the war. I.e., the post-war upsurge represents a prolonged but temporary stock-adjustment response to an undesired depletion of the stock of children due to the war. To test this hypothesis we will probably have to wait several decades. A second explanation would be to take the Becker position that the long run relationship is a positive one, but that rapid changes in other factors that influence births, notably infant mortality and the adoption of modern birth control techniques, tended to more than offset the positive effect of the growth of income per capita between 1900 and the 1930's. Once the effect of these largely non-economic factors have worked themselves out, the number of births will rise with the standard of living.

However elegant such simple propositions may seem to the economic theorists, one doubts that the above-mentioned factors alone were strong enough to account for the remarkably rapid decline in Norwegian births. There may in addition have been other forces at work, for instance a cohort effect. That is to say, tastes regarding the desired number of children per marriage may change from one marriage cohort to another independently of income. Such a hypothesis is consistent with empirical evidence bearing on the changes in completed family size that took place during the first forty years of the 20th century in Norway.

TABLE II-9

MARRIAGES WITH DURATION TWENTY YEARS BY NUMBER OF CHILDREN
1920-1960*

Total	1920	1930	1946	1950	1960
0-1 child	13.5**	18.1	30.2	32.5	27.2
2-3 children	19.6	27.7	42.3	43.6	50.6
4 children	11.5	13.2	11.3	10.9	12.0
5 or more	55.4	41.0	16.2	13.0	10.2
	100.0	100.0	100.0	100.0	100.0
Rural					
0-1 child	12.5	15.4	24.8	26.2	21.8
2-3 children	17.2	24.4	41.5	42.8	46.2
4 children	11.2	12.9	13.1	13.3	15.7
5 or more	59.1	47.3	20.6	17.7	16.3
	100.0	100.0	100.0	100.0	100.0
Urban					
0-1 child	15.4	24.5	44.3	45.2	32.5
2-3 children	25.2	35.4	44.4	45.1	54.8
4 children	12.3	13.7	6.9	6.1	8.4
5 or more	47.1	26.4	4.4	3.6	4.3
	100.0	100.0	100.0	100.0	100.0

* Sources of data: [A24], Table 3, p. 8.
** Figures are percentages.

As is shown in Table II-9, the number of children per family changed very rapidly from marriage cohort to marriage cohort during the period in question. This table refers to the relative distribution of children of marriages of twenty years duration. In other words, the figures for 1920 refer to the marriage cohort of 1900, the data for 1930 refer to the marriage cohort of 1910 and so on. Such comparisons show that over two-thirds of the people who married in 1900 had four children or more after twenty years of marriage, and over half had five children or more. In contrast, in the 1930 cohort, over three-fourths had three children or less while the relative number of marriages that had five children or more after twenty years of union was reduced to thirteen percent.

The very rapid changes that took place within a twenty-five to thirty year period were not confined to urban marriages. A comparison of for example the 1900 with the 1926 rural marriage cohorts shows very marked changes as well. Out of those married in 1900 over seventy percent had four children or more, while those married only twenty-six years later this figure was reduced by more than one-half. In contrast, two-thirds of the 1926 rural marriage cohort had three children or less after twenty years of marriage.

The marriage cohorts of 1926 and 1930 got married during years of relatively high unemployment rates, and the level of measured unemployment in the 1920's and early 1930's was among the highest ever recorded in Norway. That may conceivably have influenced the choice as to the desired number of children for these cohorts, and measures such as aggre-

gate income per capita are not sensitive to such events. But the reduction in completed family size was so marked as far as these cohorts
were concerned that one suspects that additional, perhaps largely non-
economic, forces were at work as well.

The following conclusions may be warranted. A very simple hypothesis relating changes in aggregate per capita income with the changes
in the birth rate in a unique way should probably be rejected as an explanation of the Norwegian decline in fertility. The advances of per
capita income that accompanied the industrialization process and the
transformation of the economy was probably a necessary but not sufficient condition for this change. However, it cannot explain the exact
timing of the decline nor the rapidity of it. For example, industrialization, rural-urban migration and the growth of income was at least as
rapid in the 1890's as in the inter-war period, yet the most marked
changes in family size occurred in the latter period. Modern methods of
birth control techniques were well known in the latter half of the nineteenth century. If such technical advances were the main cause of the
rapid change in family size, we have to explain why they were adopted on
a major scale after World War I rather than before this time. It would
take a major study to identify exactly how these interrelated factors
operated; i.e., one would need studies not only on how benefits and costs
connected with children change with rapid industrialization and changing
per capita income, but also on how tastes changed and how contraceptive
knowledge was accepted and adopted among different social and income
groups.

CHAPTER III

SIMPLE AGGREGATE ECONOMETRIC MODELS OF PRE-INDUSTRIAL BIRTHS

AND MARRIAGES IN A CLOSED POPULATION

> "..., the reward of labour must neces-
> sarily encourage in such a manner the
> marriage and multiplication of labourers,
> as may enable them to supply that con-
> tinually increasing demand by a continu-
> ally increasing population.... It is
> in this manner that the demand for men,
> like that for any other commodity, nec-
> essarily regulates the production of
> men; quickens it when it goes on too
> slowly, and stops it when it advances
> too fast."
>
> Adam Smith.
> An Inquiry into the Nature and Causes of
> the Wealth of Nations.
> New York: Modern Library ed., 1937, p. 80.

III-1. Introduction

In a recent survey article on historical demography Eversley stated
that: "Of the three short-term regulators of population, marriage is the
most sensitive to economic change, birth the second, and death the least"
[B18], page 39. The literature abounds with similar statements. The
purpose of this chapter is to see how well such general economic hypotheses apply to the pre-industrial Norwegian experience.

We will confine our analysis to births and marriages. Deaths will
only be taken indirectly into consideration via the influence variations
in mortality may have on the age-structure of the population in a given

year. In Section III-2 we will briefly discuss some of the a priori considerations that lead us to expect covariation between births, marriages and economic conditions in the short run.

In Section III-3.1 I propose simple aggregate models of births and marriages. This approach differs somewhat from previous attempts in this area. The methodology of such studies has been to eliminate the trend from the dependent variable and then proceed to compute simple correlation coefficients as a measure of covariance. We feel that it may be more revealing to construct models which are aimed at predicting year to year fluctuations as well as longer swings and the trend. Both economic and demographic variables enter as arguments in our birth and marriage functions.

Finally, in Sections III-3.2 and III-3.3 we confront our a priori hypotheses with the facts. Our test method is linear regression analysis, and the empirical results are discussed in some detail.

III-2. Relations Between Births, Marriages and
Economic Conditions in the Short Run

Both the long run levels of nuptiality and fertility changed very little in Norway before 1865. For example, the percentage of ever-married women showed virtually no change between 1801 and 1865. The stability in nuptiality appears to reflect a corresponding stability in general marital fertility.[1] We have then no need to explain whether marriages and births take place but only when they do.

----

[1]The reader is referred to the discussion regarding this point in Chapter II above, especially Section II-2.2.1.

2.1. Marriages

The starting assumption is that the decision of whether to and
when to marry is a voluntary and reasonably controlled one. For most
people the basic marriage decision is closely related to expected future
prospects of providing for a family according to a desired standard of
living. It is hypothesized that these future expected prospects vary
positively with current economic conditions. That is, given that a couple have decided to marry, the timing of the union will be a function of
current economic conditions. The exact mechanism involved will of course
vary with the time, place and type of occupation of the prospective bride-
groom.

In pre-industrial societies relatively dependent on the state of
the grain harvest, a well-known argument simply states that short run
economic conditions depend largely on the yield of the harvest. If the
harvest yields a surplus of food well beyond the minimum subsistence level,
this surplus will be used by the peasants to enter into marriage which
they otherwise would have postponed. Implicitely the decision to marry
is thus viewed as any other investment decision which is dependent on some
form of saving or wealth. The exact mechanism involved presumably varies
with the structure of the economy.

One version relies mainly on the "income effect" of the harvest. If
the economic setup is such that most people produce their own grain, or
alternatively that wages are paid in terms of grain, a good harvest will
increase income in the society. A second version of the harvest hypothesis
runs mainly in terms of "the price effects" of abundant or deficient har-

vests. This version implicitly assumes that grain is bought and sold in a market. And since grain in the form of bread is the most important consumer item, the "consumer price index" is largely determined by this single price. Furthermore, since the demand for food (bread) is price inelastic, prices will vary inversely with supply in the short run. Thus if nominal wages remain relatively stable, real wages will be determined by short-run fluctuations in grain prices. What is often left out of this argument, however, is the price effect on the sellers of grain, who clearly would be adversely affected by a fall in its price given the implicitly assumed price elasticity of demand. Thus for a price fall to result in significant increases in real income in the society the group of sellers must be assumed to be small in number or already so wealthy that they are insensitive to price fluctuations. For the time period for which we have data, I will test the hypothesis that grain prices were inversely related to aggregate marriages.

For the harvest to be the sole determinant of economic conditions the economy must be assumed to be a closed one. As was briefly described in Chapter II, Norwegians were engaged in foreign trade in the eighteenth century. The export trades grew rapidly during the following century, and the foreign exchange earnings helped pay for imports of grain. Furthermore, many peasants had part-time employment connected with the export trades. In such an economy short-run economic conditions will depend not only on the domestic harvest but in addition on the foreign demand for exportables and the foreign excess supply of grain. It is beyond the scope of the present paper to construct a model that explains

the pre-industrial business cycle in Norway. Rather, economic conditions
will be assumed to be given exogenously. We hypothesize that the relevant economic variable to focus on is aggregate employment conditions.
Below I will test the hypothesis that marriages were partly determined
by employment conditions in the short run.

2.2. Births

We now turn briefly to the question of to what extent births were
regulated by short-run fluctuations in economic conditions. Or more specifically, given that new marriages and the resulting births of these
have a tendency to vary positively with economic conditions in the short
run, are there any a priori reasons why births of established marriages
should do the same? This last question turns partially on the extent to
which marital fertility was actively controlled even in a pre-industrial
setting. That is, if we can assume that voluntary control prevailed, it
would be rational for a married couple to postpone an additional birth
until adverse economic conditions improved and vice versa. But can we
realistically make such an assumption?

Writers like Himes [B27] have suggested that birth control has always been practiced. In the countryside, everyone was supposed to know
one old woman who could prescribe a herbal infusion to promote miscarriage,
or to interfere more actively to produce an abortion. In her work on
pre-industrial population movements in Sweden, Dorothy Thomas claims that
voluntary birth control was practiced and that variations in contraceptive
usage prevailed. See [B69], page 85. Other students of pre-industrial
populations doubt the importance of widespread voluntary use of contra-

ception.   In a very thorough study Ohlin argues that: "As Norman Himes
has shown, techniques for contraception have been known in all societies
and at all times, but it is an entirely different proposition to assert
that they were sufficiently general and sufficiently effective to reduce
marital fertility." [B55], pages 188-189. He concludes: "That acute
contemporary observers should have made no reference to voluntary birth
restriction, had it been prevalent, is not impossible, but is unlikely."
Ibid., page 191. As far as we know, no additional evidence applying
specifically to the Norwegian case exists. In light of this we prefer
not to make any strong assumption on the extent of the prevalence and dif-
fusion of contraceptive techniques in pre-industrial Norway. This lack
of knowledge need not destroy a hypothesis of a connection between economic condition and a rational spacing of births. Even if contraceptive
techniques were not known, voluntary and temporary abstention from marital relations would be one obvious and very simple way of accomplishing
this objective.

     A second set of factors are involuntary and physiological in nature.
But the reasons are ultimately connected with the adequacy of the harvest
and the food supply. In order to argue that this factor may work in addition to the voluntary control of births, assume for the moment that any
sort of birth control is nonexistent and that the number of conceptions
remains constant from year to year. Even under modern conditions gyne-
cologists estimate that one in four or five conceptions fails to produce
a live birth. The proportion was probably higher in a "normal" year in
the past. The key to this argument is that in abnormal years in a pre-

industrial society, either exceptionally good or bad, this proportion
would vary a good deal. That is, an inadequate harvest would contribute
to a smaller proportion of a given number of conceptions leading to live
births. This biological argument goes one step further and says that
the number of conceptions would also be affected for physiological
reasons in abnormal years.

In our empirical tests below it will of course be impossible to
single out the separate effects of voluntary and involuntary factors
that affect aggregate births. However, since the "physiological hypothesis" should apply largely to abnormal years we will attempt to measure
the impact of such years on births by the use of dummy variables.

III-3. The Models and the Regression Results

I will now attempt to formalize some of the arguments of the previous section. First I present the basic hypotheses in the form of test-
able models. Then I turn to a discussion of the major empirical results.

3.1. The Basic Hypotheses

$$(3.1.1) \quad B_t = f(M_{t-i} \; ; \; EC_{t-j} \; ; \; nSMF_{xt-k})$$

$$(3.1.2) \quad M_t = g(EC_{t-l} \; ; \; oSUMF_{xt-m})$$

where B = births,

M = marriages,

EC = economic condition,

SMF   =   stock of married females,

SUMF   =   stock of unmarried females,

t   =   time period in years,

i,j,k,l,m =   indicators of the respective lags in years,

n,x,o =   are indexes indicating which age-groups of females
            we refer to.

In words equation (3.1.1) states that the aggregate number of births in each year is a function of three separate factors. First of all it is hypothesized that economic condition in period t-j will influence births. The exact lag j is hard to specify on a priori theoretical grounds. Since our time unit t refers to years, and since the mean "gestation period" for a birth is around nine months we specify that j will be equal to or greater than one year. Since we want to measure the short-run impact of economic conditions on births we restricted ourselves to values of j less than or equal to 3 in the empirical tests that are reported below.

The two remaining variables in the birth function may be categorized as demographic although both may depend in part on past economic events as these influenced demographic developments. The stock of married females between the ages x and x+n depends on the number of births that took place between time t-k-(x+n) and t-k-x and the mortality and nuptiality experience of these cohorts up to time t-k. The present model does not attempt to explain the variable nSMFx. Rather it is assumed to be given from "outside the system" at time t-k. Thus we are specifying the past female birth and age-specific mortality and nuptiality experience as predetermined variables for the purpose of analyzing their joint effect on present births.

As the third separate factor influencing births we included new marriages. The reason is that these are allegedly much more fertile than established ones. This variable will of course only affect first-order births. Unfortunately the pre-industrial birth data cannot be separated into first and higher order births. We will therefore have to specify the nature of the lag i. Clearly i has to be less than k since we want to measure the separate effect of new marriages as opposed to established ones. Yet i has to be long enough to allow for conception and a normal pregnancy period. Is there any typical or normal lag between marriage and the first birth? Eversley states that: "Where we have information, it appears that the interval between marriage and the first intramaritally conceived birth is usually between fifteen and eighteen months,...." [B18], page 47. The exact statistical meaning of "usually between fifteen and eighteen months" is not specified. If we can take this statement to mean that the mean lag is between sixteen and seventeen months we would also like to know the variance around this mean. In our empirical work we will try slightly different lags which are consistent with the two considerations just mentioned.

The marriage function (3.1.2) is analytically quite analogous to the birth function we have postulated. We hypothesize that the aggregate number of marriages in pre-industrial Norway was a function of the short-run fluctuations in economic condition. Furthermore it depended on the stock of unmarried females, SUMF, between the ages x and x+o specified below to be the years during which people conventionally marry. As above, it will be assumed that these two variables are predetermined.

I now proceed to specify the stochastic version of our model as a set of reduced form equations. We also list the a priori assumptions we make about the error terms. Some of these assumptions will be tested below.

(3.1.3) $Bt = a_0 + a_1 ECt-j + a_2 Mt-i + a_3 nSMFxt-k + Ut$

(3.1.4) $Mt = b_0 + b_1 ECt-1 + b_2 oSUMFxt-m + Vt$

Exogenous variables: ECt-j; ECt-1

Predetermined variables: nSMFxt-k; oSUMFxt-m; Mt-i

Endogenous variables: Bt, Mt

Disturbance terms: Ut, Vt

The properties of the disturbance terms are specified as follows:

(a) $E(Ut) = 0; E(Vt) = 0$ for all t

(b) $\begin{aligned} E(Ut \cdot Ut+s) \\ E(Vt \cdot Vt+s) \end{aligned} = \begin{cases} 0 \text{ for } S \neq 0 \text{ and for all } t \\ \sigma^2 \text{ for } S = 0 \text{ and for all } t \end{cases}$

(c) $E(Ut \cdot Vt-i) = 0$ for all t and i

In words the first assumption states that the U's and the V's are random variables with zero expectation. The second one says that both the U's and the V's separately have constant variance (homoscedacity) and that both the U's and the V's are pairwise uncorrelated. Finally, assumption (c) states that Ut is uncorrelated with the value of V in time period t-i.

Since Mt-i enters in equation (3.1.3) we need this last assumption in order for an ordinary least square estimator (OLS) to give us consistent estimates of it. It does not seem to be, a priori, a very strong assumption. However, we will return to it when we discuss the estimates. We therefore turn to that task.

As has been alluded to previously, yearly data that represents what we broadly defined as economic condition is scarce in Norway before 1865. We have been able to construct a yearly index of economic conditions back to 1845. Before this time we possess yearly data on agricultural prices back to 1820 in addition to qualitative estimates of exceptional harvest yields. We also carried the age-structure data, available on a yearly basis after 1845, back to the census of 1801 with the aid of the intermediate census figures. Before this time we were not able to obtain even age-structure figures. The tests of our model will therefore be confined to the period 1801-1865. First we apply the model to the period 1801-1845. Then we compare the results with the tests for the period 1845-1865 for which yearly data on economic conditions exists.[2]

3.2. The Regression Results for the Period 1801-1845

Due to the data constraints referred to immediately above, I only attempted to estimate the following equation for the period before 1845:

$$(3.2.1) \quad B_t = a_0 + a_1 M_{t-1} + a_3 \ 30\,SMF\,20 \ t-1 + U_t$$

---

[2]All the data sources used for the regression analysis carried out in this chapter can be found in Appendix A. Wherever we constructed data from primary statistical material, the methods used are briefly described.

The results are set forth in Table III-1. However, before I turn to a discussion of the empirical results, I will briefly describe the meaning of the statistics reported in this table along with the use which will be made of these in making inferences about the various hypotheses set forth. This notation will be used throughout the remainder of this study; however, the reader who is already familiar with the somewhat cryptic statistical conventions employed may want to skip the following paragraphs.

$\bar{R}^2$ is the conventional coefficient of determination corrected for degrees of freedom and is a measure of goodness of fit. F refers to the corresponding F- statistic which I use to test the null-hypothesis of no relationship between the endogenous variable and the whole set of explanatory variables. Asterisks attached to the estimated F- statistic represents levels of significance; a single asterisk means "significant at the 5% level", a double asterisk means "significant at the 1% level". That is to say, it represents the probability levels at which we can reject the null-hypothesis or accept the whole model as our maintained hypothesis. When the asterisk is absent we cannot reject the null-hypothesis at the 5% level.

The t-statistics reported in column (3) refer to the estimated regression coefficients reported in column (2) divided by the respective estimated standard errors. Asterisks attached to the t-values have the exact same meaning as above except that it now refers to hypotheses tests carried out on each individual regression coefficient. When economic theory postulates a priori the sign of the regression coefficient, either positive or negative, we will carry out one-tailed hypothesis tests on the coefficients. When our theory does not indicate in advance what sign to expect the test will be a two-tailed one. The partial correlation coefficient listed in column (5) are measures of the correlation between the dependent variable and the one specified independent variable when the linear influence of all the other independent variables on the dependent variable is eliminated. This statistic squared, or the partial $\bar{r}^2$'s exhibited in column (4), measures the proportion of the variation in the dependent variable that is explained by the independent variable in question when we have standardized for or "taken out" the influence of the remaining independent variables in the equation. Thus this is the statistical equivalent of the economic theorists's technique of impounding certain variables in a <u>ceteris</u> <u>paribus</u> clause.[3]

Finally, we have also calculated the Durbin-Watson statistic D.W. to test for the absence of autocorrelation in the disturbances. This amounts to the same thing as testing the first part of assumption (b) about the error terms above. Again, asterisks are used to indicate if the hypothesis of no serial correlation in the disturbance terms can be accepted.[4]

---

[3]For further details on the meaning of this statistic, the reader is referred to Johnston [B34], section 2-5, pages 58-61.

[4]In a general model of the form:
$y = c_1 x_1 + c_2 x_2 + \ldots c_t x_t + e$ the null-hypothesis
H_0 is that : $\varrho = 0$ against the alternative hypothesis
H_1 : $\varrho > 0$
in the stationary Markov process
$e_i = \varrho e_{i-1} + f_i$ where
ϱ is the serial correlation coefficient of the error terms specified to be $|\varrho| < 1$. If t is large it can be shown that the relationship between

TABLE III-1

REGRESSION RESULTS OF BIRTH MODEL 3.2.1

Dependent Variable Bt. Sample Period 1801-1845, N=45
Estimation Method: Ordinary Least Squares (OLS)

(1) Independent Variables	(2) Regression Coefficients	(3) t-Ratios	(4) Partial $\bar{r}^2$	(5) Partial r
Constant Term	-20680.0			
Mt-1	2.071	5.3015**	0.3809	0.6172
30 SMF 20 t-1	0.2829	5.4749**	0.4761	0.6900

$\bar{R}^2 = 0.8551$; F 100.0** ; D.W = 1.463

With these preliminaries out of the way we turn to a discussion
of the regression results. At first sight the results exhibited in
Table III-1 appear very promising. Our simple model (3.2.1) is able
to explain over 85 percent of the variation in births, and the individual regression coefficients have the correct signs and are different from zero at the 1% significance level. However, the partial regression coefficient of marriages on births, $\partial Bt/\partial Mt-1$, is implausibly

---

ϱ and the Durbin-Watson statistic D.W. is:
    D.W. $\approx$ 2 - 2ϱ and
    plim D.W. = 2 - 2ϱ thus
    0 $\leq$ D.W. $\leq$ 4
If for example $\hat{\varrho}$ = 0, then D.W. = 2, etc. Asterisk on the computed
Durbin-Watson statistic indicates, then, the probability with which we
can accept the null-hypothesis H_0 that ϱ = 0. Conversely, absence of
asterisks indicates that we cannot accept the null-hypothesis which means
that our assumption that successive error terms are uncorrelated is, for
one reason or another, invalid. For more details consult the original
articles by Durbin and Watson [A12].

large. It is highly unlikely that each new marriage produced over 2
births between time periods t-1 and t. A couple that married at the
beginning of year t-1 may of course produce 2 children by the end
of the year t, and some couples may have twins, but this should be offset by couples that did not have children at all. We therefore suspect that the estimated regression coefficient is biased upwards. The
reason that comes immediately to mind is that the regression is underspecified due to the lack of economic data. Thus the marriage variable
"picks up" not only the effect of new marriages on births but also some
of the effect of the left out variable, namely economic conditions.[5]
Such a hypothesis is consistent with the estimated Durbin-Watson statistic. The numerical value of D.W. indicates that the error terms may
be serially correlated which may mean that one important explanatory
variable is missing in the estimated equation.

We attempted to add grain prices to model (3.2.1) but the results
were disappointing. The regression coefficient of grain prices lagged
one period with respect to births had a negative sign, but the estimated
standard error of this coefficient was very large resulting in a t-
statistic close to zero in absolute value. From this fact we have to
reject the hypothesis that grain prices have any influence on births
during the sample period. One reason for this result may be of course
that our statistics on grain prices are very incomplete and that the figures we have are poor indicators of the "true" fluctuations in consumer

---

[5]For a rigorous exposition on how underspecification may lead to
biased estimates of the regression coefficients, see Theil [A37].

prices at the time. But for lack of better data we cannot pursue this line of reasoning further. Instead we propose a different test of the "harvest hypothesis."

This version of the general harvest theory is briefly as follows. In a year of "normal" harvest yields, defined very roughly as years where there is neither any acute shortage nor surplus of food, other factors determine the number of births. That is to say, in such years harvests have no appreciable influence on demographic phenomena. However, when there is either considerable excess demand for or excess supply of agricultural production, such economic phenomena will influence the short-run behavior of births. To test such a hypothesis we employed dummy variables as follows. In years which are described in the qualitative literature on Norwegian economic history for the period 1801-1845 as "bad" or "exceptionally bad" we enter a dummy variable, d, as -1 indicating that we expect economic conditions in such years to affect births negatively. In all other years $d = 0$. Conversely, in years described as "very good" or "abundant in yield", a dummy variable c is entered as +1. In all other years $c = 0$. The regression results of this modification of our basic model are set forth as model (3.2.2) in Table III-2.[6]

It is felt that model 3.2.2 is an improvement over model 3.2.1 in several respects. Particularly, both dummy variables d and c are significantly different from zero at the 1% level indicating that years

---

[6]It is clear that the results that follow depend on the characterization of years as "good" and "bad". The a priori reasons for the characterization of years as based on previous work in Norwegian economic history of the period is discussed in the appendix to this chapter. See Appendix A.

TABLE III-2

REGRESSION RESULTS OF BIRTH MODELS 3.2.2 AND 3.2.3

Dependent Variable Bt.   Sample Period 1801-1845, N=45
Estimation Method: OLS

Panel A: Birth Model 3.2.2

(1) Independent Variables	(2) Regression Coefficients	(3) t-Ratios (40)	(4) Partial $\bar{r}^2$	(5) Partial r
Constant Term	-17950.0			
Mt-1	2.286	13.6731**	0.8061	0.8978
SMFt-1	0.2515	12.7028**	0.7815	0.8840
d	3314.0	9.4531**	0.6599	0.8123
c	2402.0	6.9183**	0.4992	0.7065

$\bar{R}^2 = 0.9731$; $F > 100.0^{**}$; D.W = 1.8014**
$\quad\quad\quad\quad\quad\quad$ (4,40)

Panel B: Birth Model 3.2.3

(1) Independent Variables	(2) Regression Coefficients	(3) t-Ratios (39)	(4) Partial $\bar{r}^2$	(5) Partial r
Constant Term	-16670.0			
Mt-1	2.243	15.7064**	0.8460	0.9198
SMFt-1	0.2468	14.5973**	0.8255	0.9086
dd	5273.0	9.2186**	0.6451	0.8032
d	2742.0	8.2831**	0.5911	0.7688
c	2433.0	8.2241**	0.5874	0.7664

$\bar{R}^2 = 0.9805$; $F > 100.0^{**}$; D.W = 1.8539**

of exceptional agricultural output had very significant impacts upon the number of births. It appears, furthermore, that $\partial B/\partial d$ is considerably larger than $\partial B/\partial c$. In other words, the average impact of "bad years" was much larger in numerical value than the impact of "good years". Does this mean that large fluctuations in agricultural output around its mean value had a quantitatively asymmetrical effect on demographic phenomena? And if so, what caused this?

In order to pursue this question a little further we asked ourselves if it were possible to distinguish between merely "bad years" and years which consisted not only of harvest failures but during which additional adverse factors led to extremely harsh economic conditions. Thus for such events to occur harvest failures were a necessary but not sufficient condition. When such years were recorded, a dummy variable dd was entered = -1. Otherwise dd was set equal to zero. We refer to this addition to our previous model as model (3.2.3) and report the regression calculations in panel B of Table III-2.

The results lead one to accept the hypothesis that $|dd| > |d|$. Both dummy variables are highly significant and $\partial B/\partial dd$ is almost twice as large as $\partial B/\partial dd$. These regression coefficients give us a quantitative measure of the additional effect on births of the disruption of economic activity that events like wars had over and above the effect of harvest failures. The pre-industrial Norwegian birth-pattern may have been especially vulnerable to such disruptions due to her dependence on large imports of food, mainly grain. The exact cause of this additional effect is harder to pin down. It is very likely, however, that in such years other factors than voluntary restrictions of births were involved. Disease and physiological deteriation may have caused involuntary abortions and reduction in actual fertility in these years.[7]

A further finding of model (3.2.3) is that, aside from disaster years, the quantitative impact of "good" and "bad" years appears to be fairly symmetrical. That is, $\partial B/\partial d$ is now not much larger in absolute value than $\partial B/\partial c$. According to this result, years of abundant agricultural output provided savings that allowed couples to catch up with child production that had been deficient during bad years. Such an interpretation implies that the timing of births was subject to voluntary control even in a pre-industrial setting. This last implication cannot, of course, be proven directly. But it seems implausible, at least to this student, that medical factors alone can explain the marked fluctuations in births in "non-disaster" years.

As our maintained hypothesis for the period 1801-1845 we adopt model (3.2.3) as an improvement over (3.2.2). This function explains more than 98 percent of the variance in year to year fluctuations in births over the whole period. Furthermore, the value of the computed Durbin-Watson statistic now indicates that we can accept the hypothesis of no serial correlation in the residuals. This means that the computed standard errors are unbiased estimates which in turn give us unbiased

---

[7]The dummy variable dd was entered only in 1813 and 1814, and refers to economic conditions in 1812 and 1813. These were years not only of bad harvests following previous years of bad harvests, but they were in addition afflicted by disruptions in trade caused by the Napoleonic wars. However, there are no reports of extensive outbreaks of epidemics similar to the ones found during the "dismal peak years" in 1740-1742 and 1771-1773.

t- statistics. The partial regression coefficients $\partial B/\partial Mt-1$ and
$\partial B/\partial SMFt-1$ in model (3.2.3) have changed little compared to the estimates in model (3.2.1). The corresponding elasticities of marriages
and age-structure with respect to births were computed and found to be
0.5657 and 0.9622 respectively. Thus a one percent increase in the
stock of married females had almost twice the relative impact on births
compared to a one percent increase in new marriages. However, we still
suspect the estimate of $\partial B/\partial Mt-1$ to be biased upward. The reason for
this possibility was given when we discussed model (3.2.1). The only
way we know of to throw additional light on the nature of this bias is
to apply our basic birth model to the period 1846-1865 for which we
have yearly data on both new marriages and economic conditions.

3.3 Regression Results for the Period 1846-1865

In this section I will report and discuss the results of empirical
tests of several variants of the basic birth and marriage functions set
forth in Section 3.1.referring to the years 1846-1865. For this period
I have constructed an empirical proxy for short-run variations in economic conditions, referred to as EC, based on poor relief data.[8] The results of fitting several variants of the basic birth function are exhibited in Table III-3.

The complete birth model, i.e. model 3.3.1, is exhibited in panel A
of this table. It is seen that our basic birth hypothesis holds up well.
The three independent variables together account for almost 90 percent of

---

[8]For more details, see Appendix A.

TABLE III-3

105

REGRESSION RESULTS OF BIRTH MODELS 3.3.1, 3.3.2 AND 3.3.3

Dependent Variable: Bt. Sample Period 1846-1865.
Estimation Method: OLS

Panel A: Birth Model 3.3.1

(1) Independent Variables	(2) Regression Coefficients	(3) t-Ratios (16)	(4) Partial $\bar{r}^2$	(5) Partial r
Constant Term	24100			
Mt-1	1.501	1.9764*	0.0455	0.2133
EC	-432.2	2.2447*	0.0969	0.3113
SMFt-1	0.1819	6.5438**	0.6770	0.8228

$\bar{R}^2$ = 0.8945 ; F = 54.68** ; D.W = 1.9505**
                    (4;16)

Panel B: Birth Model 3.3.2

(1) Independent Variables	(2) Regression Coefficients	(3) t-Ratios (17)	(4) Partial $\bar{r}^2$	(5) Partial r
Constant Term	17793			
Mt-1	2.323	3.1395**	0.2925	0.5408
SMFt-1	0.2095	7.5642**	0.7440	0.8626

$\bar{R}^2$ = 0.8694 ; F = 64.23** ; D.W = 1.5664**
                    (3;17)

Panel C: Birth Model 3.3.3

(1) Independent Variables	(2) Regression Coefficients	(3) t-Ratios	(4) Partial $\bar{r}^2$	(5) Partial r
Constant Term	44610			
EC	-615.7	3.3741**		0.5750
SMFt-1	0.1930	6.5527**		0.8264

$\bar{R}^2$ = 0.8764 ; F = 68.37** ; D.W = 1.7977**
                    (3;17)

the yearly variations in births. This is quite comparable to the fits
for the period before 1846. The age-structure variable is, furthermore,
significantly different from zero at the 1% level of probability with
a regression coefficient similar to the one estimated for the previous
period. This is not the case with $\partial B/\partial Mt-1$. The regression coefficient
of new marriages on births is now reduced to 1.501 and the partial coefficient of determination $\bar{r}^2$, i.e. the proportion of the variation in
births that is explained by the addition of Mt-1, is now quite small.
See column 4 in Table III-3, panel A. The same applies to the index of
variations in economic condition EC. The regression coefficient of this
variable with respect to births has the expected sign and is statistically
significant at the 5% level, but its partial $\bar{r}^2$ is quite small too.
This fact led to the suspicion that Mt-1 and EC were highly intercorre-
lated so that their joint appearance in model 3.3.1 would effect both
estimates due to multicollinearity. I therefore examined the simple or
zero-order correlation coefficients between these two independent variables and the correlation between each individual explanatory variable
and the dependent one. See Table III-4, panel B. As can be seen from
this matrix, the estimated zero-order correlation coefficient of Mt-1
on EC is -0.651, while those of Mt-1 and EC on Bt equal 0.700 and -0.781
respectively. This finding strongly supports our initial suspicion of
strong multicollinearity between marriages and economic conditions. I
therefore proceeded to test a birth function which excludes each variable
in turn. These two separate runs are reported as Birth Models 3.3.2 and
3.3.3 in panels B and C of Table III-3.

TABLE III-4

ZERO ORDER CORRELATION COEFFICIENT MATRICES

A. Birth Model 3.2.3. Sample Period 1801-1845

	Bt	Mt-1	SMFt-1	dd	d
Mt-1	0.851				
SMFt-1	0.875	0.730			
dd	0.356	0.157	0.161		
d	0.113	-0.108	-0.036	-0.093	
c	0.364	0.049	-0.086	0.115	0.229

B. Birth Model 3.3.1. Sample period 1846-1865

	Bt	Mt-1	EC
Mt-1	0.700		
EC	-0.781	-0.651	
SMFt-1	0.903	0.531	-0.631

C. Marriage Model 3.3.5. Sample period 1846-1865

	Mt	Ut	SUMFt-1	d46	d54
ECt	-0.662				
SUMFt-1	0.568	-0.496			
d46	-0.044	0.379	-0.392		
d54	0.426	-0.098	0.004	-0.053	
d55	0.272	-0.125	-0.001	-0.053	-0.053

The results of model (3.3.2) are quite comparable to the results of model (3.2.1) in section (3.2) above both when it comes to fit and the estimates of the regression coefficients. We see also that when we drop economic condition from our computations the proportion of variation in births explained by M_{t-1} goes up to 0.3 or six times its value in model (3.3.1). However, model (3.3.3) seems preferable to model (3.3.2) for several reasons. First of all, one of the basic questions we set out to ask ourselves was whether births were related to fluctuations in economic condition. We therefore feel that we can get better answers to this question by employing a model in which this factor enters directly. Secondly, we want to quantitatively estimate the relation between the two unaffected by other variables that may bias such estimates. It is evident from model (3.3.1) that the presence of M_{t-1} did just that. To try to get around the problem of multicollinearity we attempted different lag-structures for the variable M_{t-1}. For the period 1846-1865 we tried to work with monthly data and employ various monthly lag-structures instead of just relating marriages lagged one year to births in year t. The outcome of these efforts was largely negative. In other words, we felt we were unable to confidently single out the separate effect of marriages on births by linear regression methods. This decision led to accepting model (3.3.3) as our maintained hypothesis. An additional advantage of this decision is that we no longer need assumption (c) on page 10, namely that $E(U_t \cdot V_{t-i})=0$, in order for us to be certain that the ordinary least squares estimators will give us consistent estimates of both the birth and marriage functions.

In model (3.3.3) both explanatory variables are highly statistically significant. From the estimates of the regression coefficients we computed the respective elasticities of EC and SMF t-1 with respect to births. They were found to equal -0.5701 and 0.6585 respectively. Thus a one percent change in the stock of married females has a slightly larger relative average impact on births than a corresponding change in economic condition. If we furthermore look at the proportion of variance in births explained by each individual variable ceteris paribus, the demographic variable alone can account for 68 percent of the variance in births when we hold economic factors constant. The corresponding figure for economic condition is 33 percent. Thus measured, demographic causes were "more important" than economic ones in explaining variations in births during this period. As was mentioned earlier, such a demographic variable is to a large extent determined by past fertility, mortality and nuptiality experience, which of course in turn can be partially explained by past economic events.

As a last exercise we asked ourselves if Mt-1 was significantly related to the unexplained residuals of model (3.3.3). That is to say, can past new marriages explain the residual variance in births unexplained by the stock of married females and current economic condition? To test this hypothesis we ran a regression with the residuals of model (3.3.3) as the dependent and Mt-1 as the independent variable. The results of this test turned out to be inconclusive. The explanatory marriage variable was significantly different from zero at the 10% but not at the 5% level of probability.

We now turn to tests of the basic marriage hypothesis. We started out by fitting this equation by ordinary least squares. The results are set forth in Table III-5. The basic model (3.3.4) looks promising in the sense that the F- test leads one to accept the basic relationship at the 99 percent level of significance. Furthermore, the estimated coefficients have the signs that were postulated a priori. However, we cannot reject the hypothesis that successive errors are serially correlated. This might mean underspecification in the sense that important explanatory variables have been left out. This suspicion is increased by examining more closely the economic history of the period. The first year of our sample period, 1846, was a year of "below average" grain harvest. Furthermore, the potato crop failed completely in all of the important agricultural districts. [B31], page 60. On the other hand, the mid-1850's were a boom period for the Norwegian economy. The Crimean War provided fuel for these expansion years not only for exports of lumber and shipping services but also for agriculture. Ibid., pages 67-68.

We therefore went back and examined the residuals of regression model (3.3.4), and found that these years were indeed the ones in which our basic marriage model gave relatively poor predictions. The reason for this may simply be that our indicator of economic condition is relatively insensitive to such exceptional years. Put differently, during these years economic conditions were quite abnormal so as to shift the marriage function temporarily. To test this argument, we once more employed the dummy variable technique.

TABLE III-5

REGRESSION RESULTS OF MARRIAGE MODELS 3.3.4 AND 3.3.5

Dependent Variable: Mt. Sample Period 1846-1865, N=20
Estimation Method: OLS

Panel A: Model 3.3.4

(1) Independent Variables	(2) Regression Coefficients	(3) t-Ratios (17)	(4) Partial $\bar{r}^2$	(5) Partial r
Constant Term	9378.0			
ECt	114.0	2.5904**	0.1987	
25 SUMF 15 t-1	0.0275	1.6347	0.0342	

$\bar{R}^2 = 0.4576$; F = 9.0161** ; D.W = 1.3961
(2,17)

Panel B: Model 3.3.5

(1) Independent Variables	(2) Regression Coefficients	(3) t-Ratios (14)	(4) Partial $\bar{r}^2$	(5) Partial r
Constant Term	6902.0			
ECt	-112.8	3.6376**	0.3023	0.5498
25 SUMF 15 t-1	0.0398	3.3696**	0.2506	0.5006
d 46	970.2	2.8244**	0.1355	
d 54	1094.0	3.5299**	0.2819	
d 55	673.6	2.1638*	0.0	

$\bar{R}^2 = 0.7524$; F = 12.5472** ; D.W = 1.8955**
(6,14)

During the years 1846, 1854 and 1855 the dummies d46, d54 and d55 were entered as -1, +1, and +1 respectively. In all other years these dummies were set equal to zero. The marriage model thus modified is exhibited as model (3.3.5) in Table III-5. Because of the modification, the regression results improved considerably. Firstly, the three dummies all proved to be highly significant. They provide, furthermore, a quantitative verification of the fact that nuptiality in Norway during these years was still quite sensitive to exceptional economic events. For example, the very marked adverse conditions in agriculture in 1846 reduced the number of marriages by 970 or almost 10 percent of the mean yearly figure for the period. Conversely, an exceptional boom increased nuptiality by a comparable figure over and above what our index of economic conditions and the stock of unmarried females would predict.

The estimated regression coefficients of EC_t and $SUMF_{t-1}$ did not change much by the addition of the dummies. That is, their estimates in model (3.3.5) are not much different from their (3.3.4) values. This fact verifies the suspicion that EC_t, our index of economic condition, is relatively insensitive to extreme years.[9] Neither would we expect our demographic variable to be sensitive to such changes. The inclusion of the dummies in the model reduces the estimated serial correlation in the error terms so that we now can, on the basis of the Durbin-Watson statistic, accept the hypothesis of random errors. This finding is consistent with our initial suspicion to the fact that model (3.3.4) was underspecified.

---

[9]The reason for this possibility is discussed further in the appendix in connection with the explanation of the construction of this index.

In model (3.3.5) both ECt and SUMF t-1 are significantly different from zero at the 99.5 percent level of significance. To assess
their relative impact upon marriages we computed their respective average elasticities with respect to marriages for the sample period from
the estimated regression coefficients. The numerical values of these
elasticities are -0.5438 and 0.7916 respectively. Thus an increase in
our crude index of "unemployment" of 1 percent led to a reduction in the
number of marriages of little over 0.5 percent on the average. Conversely, an increase in the number of unmarried females between the ages
of 15 and 39 years by 1 percent lead to an average increase in marriages
of approximately 0.8 percent. Thus the relative impact of changes in
demographic conditions on marriages was larger than that of our index
of economic conditions. However, if we look at the partial $\bar{r}^2$'s (reported in column (4) of Table III-5), economic conditions explained a
slightly larger percentage of the total variance in marriages than our
demographic index ceteris paribus. We feel that this finding is entirely
plausible and consistent with our basic view of the determination of
marriages. Of the two factors, economic conditions exhibit more marked
short-run fluctuations and may be considered as influencing mainly the
timing of marriages. The stock of unmarried females in the ages in which
marriages typically take place will change more slowly in the short run,
being dependent on past demographic factors as discussed above.

III-4. Conclusions

In order to study the interrelations between economic and demographic phenomena in a largely pre-industrial economy we constructed simple aggregate models of births and marriages as functions of economic and demographic condition. Confronted with empirical tests applying pre-1865 Norwegian data our models predicted the actual year to year movements in births and marriages quite well.

Both economic and demographic conditions proved to be highly significant explanatory variables of births and marriages while each variable alone only provided an incomplete or partial explanation of the birth and nuptiality experience of the period. Thus by constructing models which are subject to quantitative tests we found that earlier writers who stress one factor to the exclusion of the other tell us only part of the story.

For the period after 1845 we had to exclude new marriages from our initial birth function. Because of the high intercorrelation between marriages and the index of economic condition, the ordinary least squares estimates of the partial regression coefficient of each variable were impaired. Thus we were unable to separate out the independent effect of new marriages on births for this period. The pre-1845 birth regression results should be interpreted in light of this fact. The estimated partial regression coefficient of lagged marriages with respect to births includes not only the direct effect of marriages on births, but also the impact of economic condition on births.

Year to year fluctuations in grain prices were found not to exert any significant influence on births. However, harvest yields which deviated substantially from its mean in the sense that contemporaries characterized them as exceptional were found to exert a statistically significant influence on births the following year. We measured such events to have an _independent_ quantitative impact on births in either direction which amounted to almost 10 percent of the mean value of births during the period. In two years which were marked not only by harvest failures but by interruptions in trade due to wars, this figure doubled.

Finally, we tested the marriage function on data for the last 20 years of the period. Marriages in year t were found to be the most sensitive to economic conditions in the same year rather than a lagged three-year moving average as was the case with births. The economic variable explained, _ceteris paribus_, a higher percent of the total variance of marriages than the demographic index. With births the opposite was the case. Defined thus, our little cleometric exercise confirmed Eversley's flat statement that marriages are "more sensitive" to short-term economic change than births in the Norwegian pre-industrial economy.

It seems appropriate to end on a cautious note. Even though the results we arrived at may be considered surprisingly good, the reader is duly reminded that the data we have worked with must be considered quite crude by modern standards. For example, we have no way of appraising the accuracy of the economic indicators before 1865 because economic data is so scarce. The yearly age-structure data employed before 1845 is based on interpolations between census figures. Thus we may have smoothed away some of the year to year fluctuations in mortality. If this is so, some of the more extreme fluctuations in deaths may have been "picked up" by the dummy variables we employed. It is only hoped that such data deficiencies and others are not so large as to materially affect the major conclusions reached in this chapter.

CHAPTER IV

SOME SOCIO-ECONOMIC CHARACTERISTICS OF NORWEGIAN

MIGRANTS TO THE UNITED STATES

"In what country, except North-America
and some new colonies, do the wages of
free labour employed in agriculture,
much exceed a bare subsistence for the
labourer?"

Karl Marx.
Capital. A Critique of Political Economy. Vol. I. The Process of Capital-
ist Production. Engels ed.
Chicago: C. H. Kerr Co., 1906, p. 845.

IV-1. Introduction

The main purpose of this chapter is to provide a brief description of the migrants whose movements we purport to explain in Chapter V.
The decision concerning which characteristics should be included in this
chapter and which left out is somewhat arbitrary; after all, the manner
in which migrants respond to economic differentials is itself one of
their characteristics. However, most of the characteristics of migrants
which are significant from our point of view will be more or less closely
related to the labor market.

First we turn to qualities which have to do with the social structure of the Norwegian emigrants. Thus we review the rural-urban origin
of the emigration stream, where they settled in the United States, and how
these trends changed over time. Then we turn to characteristics which seem

most relevant to the labor market. These include age distribution, sex
mix, skill mix, industrial background, and the occupational distribution of the Norwegian-born emigrants in the U. S. Finally, we briefly
discuss the nature of the return migration from the United States to
Norway.

IV-2. Long-Run Trends in Norwegian Overseas
Emigration, 1836-1936

2.1. Aggregate Emigration

1836 marks the starting point of yearly records of Norwegian
emigration, but overseas migration before this time most probably was
very insignificant in size. Choosing 1936 as an end point is somewhat
arbitrary since the migration stream almost ceased in the 1930's[1]

To briefly assess the long-run trends in the migration stream we
dated the marked long swings and proceeded to compute trough to trough
averages between these dates, both in the absolute number of migrants
and in the rate of emigration per 1,000 of the mean domestic population
(the crude emigration rate). Both these series refer to yearly averages
and are exhibited in columns (1) and (2) in panel A of Table IV-1.

Yearly average emigration is quite small before 1845. After that
point the secular trend rises rapidly, with a marked acceleration between the second and the third long swing. The peak is reached during

---

[1]For more details on the nature of the Norwegian migration data,
see [B3], pp. 155-57; [B19], pp. 747-54 and especially [G13].

TABLE IV-1   119

Panel A.   AVERAGE VOLUME PER YEAR OF OVERSEAS NORWEGIAN EMIGRANTS TROUGH
TO TROUGH LONG SWINGS 1836-1936.

Total Absolute Number of Emigrants, Emigrants per 1000 mean
Norwegian Population, and percent of Total Emigrants Departing
for the U.S.

Time Periods	(1) Absolute Numbers	(2) Per 1000 of Population	(3) Percent Departing for the U.S.
1836-45	620	0.48	
1845-63	3.518	2.35	
1863-77	11.527	5.24	98.57
1877-97	14.045	7.06	99.41
1897-1918	12.342	5.30	93.24
1918-1936	5.207	1.90	76.76

Panel B.   RURAL-URBAN ORIGIN OF NORWEGIAN EMIGRANTS.

Average Annual Crude Rates and the Relative Number from Urban
Areas for Selected Periods.

Time Periods	(1) Rural Emigrants per 1000 of Mean Rural Population	(2) Urban Emigrants per 1000 Mean Urban Population	(3) Relative Number of Urban Emigrants in percent
1856-1865	2.77	0.72	4.40
1866-1880	5.97	6.23	18.55
1881-1900	6.40	9.28	30.53
1901-1920	4.98	6.33	33.87
1921-1935	2.00	2.60	34.77

Sources of Data:

Panel A: Col. (1) and Col. (2) computed from [G13], Table 14, pp. 42-44.
         Col. (3): 1867-1924 computed from [B19], Norway, Table IV, p. 752.
                   1925-1935 computed from [B3], Table 88, p. 159.
Panel B: Computed from [B3], Table 90, p. 164.

the long swing spanning roughly the last quarter of the 19th century.
During this swing the emigration over a 10-year period amounted to
7 percent of total population, something very large, indeed. The level
of emigration tapers off after that. The fifth swing is quite comparable to the third one. After World War I, overseas emigration falls
off rapidly only to virtually disappear in the 1930's.

2.2. Rural and Urban Emigration

Figures on direct emigration from rural and urban districts respectively are set forth in panel B of Table IV-1. We were only able to
obtain such data for quinquennial periods. From these we computed yearly
averages for subperiods that correspond closely to the long swings we
marked off in the aggregate yearly data. For the period for which we
have data, the trend patterns for both the crude rural and urban emigration rates are similar to the aggregate pattern. That is to say, a peak
is reached in the last subperiod of the 19th century after which the
level of both rural and urban emigration tapers off.

However, the urban yearly rate of emigration per thousand of the
base population lies above the rural rate in every subperiod. Can we
conclude from this that urban dwellers had a higher propensity to emigrate than their rural counterparts? Probably not. There are at least
two reasons why such a conclusion might be improper. The first one simply has to do with the deficiency of crude rates as measures of propen-
sities. In Chapter II we briefly alluded to the internal rural-urban
migration that took place during this period. Since most of these migrants most likely were in the younger ages, such internal migration

would cause the urban population to have a different age-distribution than the rural one. Crude rates do not standardize for this fact, and since we do not have separate figures on the age-distributions of the rural and urban populations respectively, we cannot compute age-specific rural and urban migration rates.

Secondly, and perhaps more importantly, these figures only tell us something about direct emigration from rural and urban areas. That is to say, a farmer who migrates to a city and works there for a while before emigrating might very well have been recorded as an urban emigrant. This raises the interesting question of to what extent emigrants from urban areas, but of rural origin, were merely transients in the city on their way to the U.S.A. The Norwegian historian, Ingrid Semmingsen, provides some information on the number of urban emigrants from Bergen (the second largest city in Norway) that were actually born in rural districts. During the time period 1875-84, 61 percent of the males and 55 percent of the females were originally from the countryside. For 1885-94 the respective percentages were 55 and 48. [B61], p. 233. She, furthermore, voices the opinion that: "two-thirds and perhaps even a larger number from the city of Oslo during the last 30 years of the 19th century were of rural origin." Ibid., p. 234. Unfortunately, there is no information on how long the urban emigrants of rural origin lived in the cities before they emigrated. To throw more light on the length of the transition period, it would have been desirable to see if urban dwellers of rural origin emigrated in greater proportion to their number in the towns than the town-dwellers of urban origin. Unfortunately, such information, to the best of my knowledge, does not exist.

2.3. The Relation Between Norwegian Internal Rural-Urban Migration and
Overseas Emigration

In relation to the above discussion one may ask if there is any
apparent systematic relationship between the pattern of internal and
overseas migration. The answer to such a question may be of considerable
interest. That is to say, if the pattern is largely inverse one might
speculate that rural dwellers migrate to a Norwegian city when industrialization and urban economic development proceeded at a rapid pace. When
such developments were punctuated or slowed, the last wave of urban migrants from rural areas will presumably be the first ones to lose their
jobs. The ones who do will then have the choice of returning to the
Norwegian countryside, or, alternatively, emigrating overseas. The pace
of urban economic growth in Norway will, if this is indeed the case,
play an important role in determining the timing of overseas departures
not only of those workers born and raised in Norwegian cities but also for
the recent rural in-migrants to these cities. For both groups the opportunity cost of traveling to the United States will, ceteris paribus, be
lower when urban employment opportunities in Norway are low. Presumably
the same argument may be applied to a third group, namely the potential
rural out-migrant who is about to decide between traveling to a Norwegian
town and emigrating overseas.

Unfortunately, internal rural-urban migration has not been recorded
directly in Norway in any comprehensive way before World War II. It was
therefore, as a first approximation, computed as a residual as follows. Between censuses we possess yearly data on natural increase in and overseas

emigration from rural districts and towns respectively. Since the net change in population in rural and urban districts can be computed from the available stock figures at each census date, internal or rural-urban migration will be the difference, either positive or negative, between natural indrease and overseas emigration on the one hand, and the net change in population on the other. The results of such computations are exhibited in Table IV-2.[2]

Perhaps the single most striking feature of Table IV-2 is the very sharp increase in net rural out-migration after 1865. (See line 4.) Before this date average yearly out-migration amounted to less than four per thousand of mean rural population. Furthermore, most of these migrants traveled overseas. In contrast, the period between 1865 and 1910 may be characterized as somewhat of a rural population exodus. For forty-five years the Norwegian rural population sustained a yearly average loss through out-migration of almost 10 per thousand, a very large figure indeed. This meant that during this period the rural areas lost forty-five

---

[2]Some care should, of course, be exercised in interpreting this residual. Even if the available data on natural increase, overseas emigration, and the stock of the Norwegian population at census dates are largely accurate, one should keep in mind that we do not have any figures on net migration between Norway and other European countries between 1846 and 1930. The way it is computed, the net balance of such Norwegian-European migration will be included in our residual. I proceed with the hope that the qualitative statements to the effect that such movements were of small magnitude and largely canceled each other out are reasonably correct. In addition, I would have liked to make Table IV-2 strictly comparable to Table II-4 in Chapter II above. That is to say, ideally we are interested in the component changes between census dates of the Norwegian population in urban and dispersed settlements as defined in Chapter II rather than in rural districts and towns for reasons given in that chapter. However, to compute such figures, if at all possible, would be a major undertaking and is beyond the scope of the present investigation.

TABLE IV-2   124

MIGRATION AND INCREASE OF POPULATION
IN RURAL DISTRICTS AND TOWNS BETWEEN CENSUS DATES
1845-1930**

Rural Districts	Time Periods							
	1846-55	1856-65	1866-75	1876-90	1891-00	1901-10	1911-20	1920-30
(1) Natural Increase	14.15*	14.90	12.58	13.87	13.24	12.93	11.35	10.72
(2) Emigration to Overseas Countries	–	-2.77	-6.85	-7.09	-4.31	-7.85	-2.19	-2.92
(3) Other Migration (Computed Residually)	–	-1.21	-2.91	-4.81	-4.60	-0.54	-0.09	-0.10
(4) Net Migration Line 2 + 3	-3.79	-3.98	-9.76	-11.90	-8.91	-8.39	-2.28	-3.02
(5) Rate of Increase of Population	10.36	10.92	2.82	1.97	4.33	4.54	9.07	7.70
Towns	**Time Periods**							
(1)	10.19	14.74	12.65	16.39	15.83	14.39	9.90	4.41
(2)	–	-0.72	-6.95	-11.32	-5.08	-9.55	-3.06	-3.77
(3)	–	+11.38	+16.91	+18.09	+19.49	+4.59	+6.20	+1.26
(4)	+8.67	+10.66	+9.96	+6.77	+14.41	-4.96	+3.14	-2.51
(5)	18.86	25.40	22.62	23.16	30.24	9.43	13.04	1.90

* All figures are average yearly rates per 1000 mean population in rural areas
and towns respectively.
** Sources of Data: For the time period 1846-65: [G2], Table No. 6, p. 173 and
                        Table No. 8, p. 184.
            For the time period 1866-75: [G5], Table 3, pp. 134-35 and
                        [B3], Table 90, p. 164.
            For the time period 1876-1930: [B3], Table 116, p. 198.

percent of its natural population increase through migration. About
one-third of this total took the form of internal or net rural-urban
migration. As a result the towns received an influx of people from
the farm areas that more than offset the fairly extensive overseas
emigration from the cities. Between 1875 and 1900 almost half of the
rural out-migrants traveled to a Norwegian city.

Unfortunately, the census dates before 1890 do not coincide
closely with the peaks and troughs in overseas Norwegian emigration as
marked off in Table IV-1, panel A. However, between 1890 and 1910 they
are much closer, and an inverse pattern between overseas emigration and
internal migration becomes apparent. That is, during the 1890's the
rate of overseas emigration is relatively low and the proportion of
rural out-migrants that traveled to a Norwegian city is high. During
the following decade the exact opposite is the case. However, it is
clear that yearly data in this respect would be more revealing. I will
now proceed to introduce additional empirical evidence that supports
the inversity hypothesis.

Starting in the 1870's we possess data on yearly net migration
into Norway's largest city, Oslo, in addition to figures on the number
of Oslo residents that emigrated overseas. Since Oslo was by far the
most important center of industrialization during the period, it may
be a good testing ground for the inversity hypothesis. If we deduct
the number of city residents who emigrated overseas in each year from
the net yearly migration figure, the residual will measure net internal
migration between Oslo and the countryside. The result of this compu-

tation is exhibited in Chart IV-1 along with the yearly movements of total overseas emigration.[3]

The major impression of Chart IV-1 is the inversity between the two series, both in the year to year fluctuations and over the long swings. Thus when the crude U.S. emigration rate increases, net emigration to Oslo, measured as the number of emigrants per 1,000 of mean Oslo population in each year, falls off rapidly or becomes negative. Such periods were: 1879-83, 1886-88, 1890-92, 1898-1903, and 1919-21. Conversely, when the flow of total emigration falls off, net emigration into the Norwegian capital rises rapidly. Such years were: 1875-79, 1883-84, 1888-90, 1893-98, 1903-08, 1914-17, and 1927-36. The correlation coefficient between the two series, computed from yearly data, is -0.550 indicating statistically significant inverse covariance between the two series.

When it comes to the long swings in both series, the inversity is perhaps more apparent. See Charts IV-2 and IV-3. For example, the long swing troughs in emigration in 1877, 1897 and the 1930's coincide closely with peaks in net internal emigration in 1878, 1898 and the 1930's. During the period between 1908 and 1916 the inversity is some-

[3]Define net migration into Oslo as NMo, emigration of Oslo residents overseas as Eus, total migration into Oslo as IMMo, and other outmigration from Oslo as OEo, then NMO = IMMo-(Eus + OEo). Rearranging we get NMo + Eus = IMMo - OEo. It is clear that the expression on the right hand side is the result of all other emigration between Oslo and other areas. Thus some of the emigrants could presumably come from other Norwegian cities rather than from the countryside. We still think that the residual may give a fairly good indication of the timing of rural-urban migration in Norway.

CHART IV-1   OVERSEAS EMIGRATION (1) AND NET MIGRATION TO OSLO (2), 1871–1937 YEARLY DATA

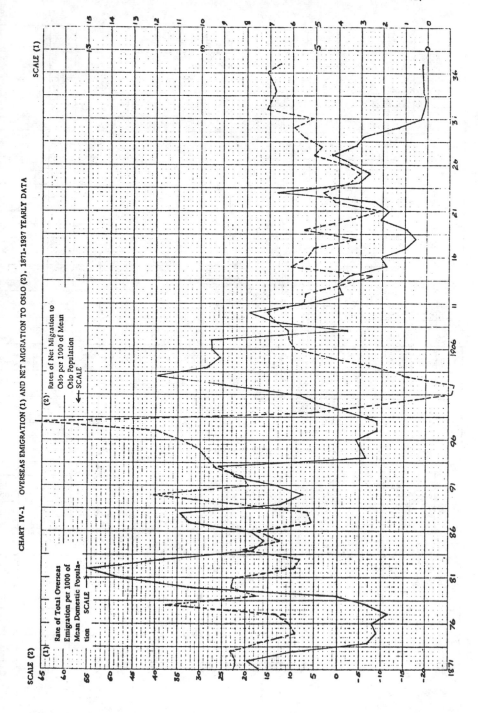

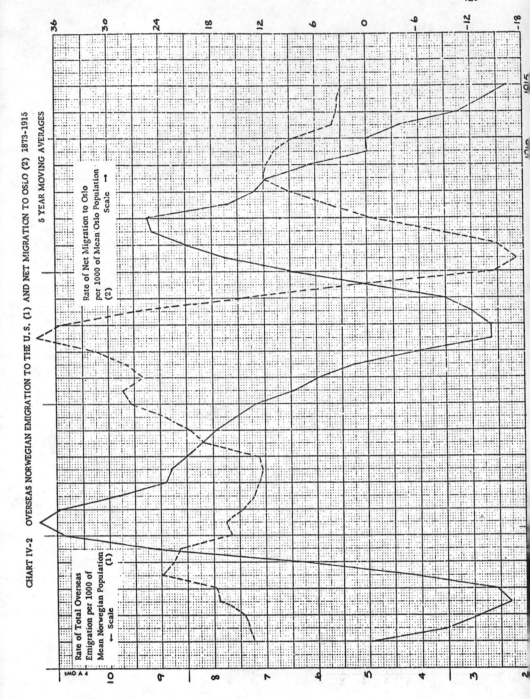

CHART IV-2   OVERSEAS NORWEGIAN EMIGRATION TO THE U.S. (1) AND NET MIGRATION TO OSLO (2) 1873-1915

5 YEAR MOVING AVERAGES

Rate of Net Migration to Oslo
per 1000 of Mean Oslo Population
(2)
Scale →

Rate of Total Overseas
Emigration per 1000 of
Mean Norwegian Population
(1)
← Scale

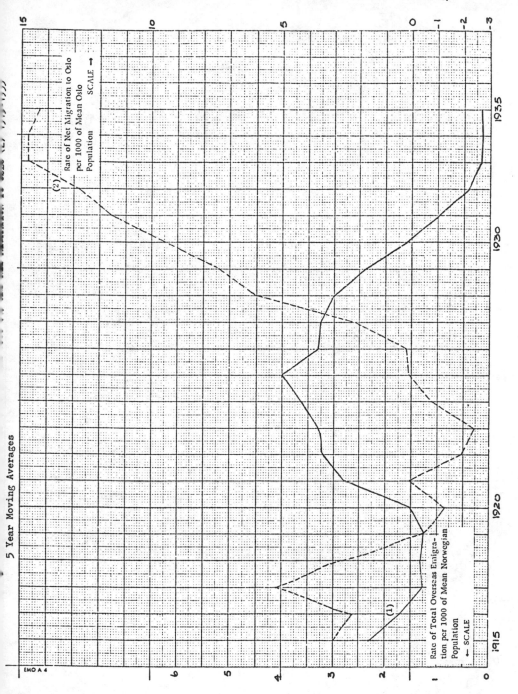

5 Year Moving Averages

(2) Rate of Net Migration to Oslo per 1000 of Mean Oslo Population   SCALE →

(1) Rate of Total Overseas Emigration per 1000 of Mean Norwegian Population   ← SCALE

EMO A 4

129

what less apparent. This may be partly because of irregularities caused by World War I. Furthermore, net overseas emigration to the U.S. during this particular period was considerably below gross outmigration because return migration from the U.S. was substantial during these years. (Return migration is discussed in more detail in section IV-6 below.)[4] If we take five-year moving averages of the yearly series, the correlation coefficient between the two is -0.639.

What can we conclude from this evidence? Consider the Norwegian economy of consisting of two sectors during the period of investigation. Assume that excess supply of labor exists in the traditional rural region and that excess demand for labor in the urban industrializing sector is determined exogenously. Variations in industrial development would in such an economy determine the pace of rural-urban migration of labor. In an open economy, defined as one in which migration to a third region or another country is feasible, employment opportunities in the domestic industrial sector would, ceteris paribus, determine the timing of emigration of both rural and urban labor because the opportunity cost of leaving the country will vary inversely with these employment opportunities. Such a "push" argument is consistent with the pattern of in-

---

[4]For the period 1890-1920 we have data on net emigration to the U.S. Compare yearly averages of the net U.S. emigration rate (NUSER) with the net internal migration rate into Oslo (NIMRO) for the following subperiods thus:

	1891-95	1896-1900	1901-05	1906-10	1910-20
NUSER:	5.73	2.84	8.29	6.16	1.36
NIMRO:	26.08	36.46	-15.03	11.98	3.13

Inverse movements are quite apparent except during the decade 1910-20.

versity between internal and external migration shown above. We will
attempt to test such a hypothesis more rigorously in Chapter V. When
we lift the _ceteris_ _paribus_ condition, we expect that variations in
excess demand for labor in the third region would also determine the
timing of emigration, along with possible variations in the excess supply of rural domestic labor. We will explore these possibilities further
in the following chapter.

IV-3. Norwegian Settlement in the United States

The U.S.A. was the destination for an overwhelming percentage of
Norwegian overseas migrants (see Table IV-1, panel A, column (3)). Even
after World War I over 75 percent of the departing emigrants listed the
U.S. as their country of destination, the remaining emigrants traveling
largely to Canada. In what parts of the U.S. did the Norwegians typically
settle? To that question we now briefly turn.[5]

Table IV-3 exhibits the distribution of Norwegian born emigrants
by principal regions at selected U.S. census dates, starting in 1850. In
reading this table, one should of course be a little careful before assuming that the difference in a region's Norwegian born population between the respective dates was entirely made up of emigrants coming di-

---

[5]This is an area that American historians have investigated quite
intensively. The reader who is interested in more historical details
than are provided in the following brief review is referred to the studies
by Blegen [B8] and Flom [B21] on the early period of Norwegian settlement.
In the period up to World War I, see the books by Bjork [B7] and Qualey
[B57].

TABLE IV-3   132

THE DISTRIBUTION OF NORWEGIAN BORN IMMIGRANTS BY PRINCIPAL REGIONS AND
SELECTED STATES AT U.S. CENSUS DATES AND CHANGES BETWEEN THESE DATES

	(1) 1850	(2) Changes 1870-1850	(3) 1870	(4) Changes 1890-1870	(5) 1890	(6) Changes 1910-1890	(7) 1910
TOTAL U.S.	12.407	101.836	114.243	206.877	321.120	80.250	401.370
NORTHEAST	550	1.195	1.745	14.339	16.084	25.048	41.132
New York	392	583	975	7.627	8.602	16.411	25.013
NORTH CENTRAL	11.580	97.816	109.396	174.451	283.847	14.131	297.978
Illinois	2.415	9.465	11.880	18.459	30.339	2.574	32.913
Wisconsin	8.651	31.395	40.046	25.650	65.696	-8.696	57.000
Minnesota	7	35.933	35.940	65.229	101.169	4.134	105.303
Iowa	361	17.193	17.554	9.524	27.078	-5.154	21.924
N-Dakota		1.179	1.179	43.851	25.773	20.164	45.937
S-Dakota					19.257	1.661	20.918
SOUTH	277	620	597	325	922	1.046	1.968
WEST	0	2.505	2.505	17.762	20.267	40.025	60.292
Montana			88	1.869	1.957	5.213	7.170
Washington			104	8.230	8.334	20.034	28.368
Oregon			76	2.195	2.271	4.572	6.843
California			1.000	2.702	3.702	6.250	9.952
TOTAL URBAN POPULATION					67.065	103.550	170.615
Selected Cities							
Chicago			6.379	15.456	21.835	2.351	24.186
Milwaukee			523	1.298	1.821	323	2.144
Minneapolis					12.624	3.778	16.402
St. Paul					3.521	542	4.063
New York			372	6.076	6.448	15.833	22.281
San Francisco			390	1.006	1.396	2.373	3.769
Seattle					1.353	5.840	7.193

Sources of Data: Col. (1) and Col. (3): [B21], Table II, pp. 385-86
Col. (5) : [G26], Part II, Tables 1 and 2, pp. 600-605
Col. (7) : [G27], Vol. I, Population Table 33, pp. 834-39.

rectly from Norway or new emigrants. The pioneers in each region of new
settlement often consisted of Norwegians that left the older settlements
to break new ground elsewhere. That often set the stage for massive
emigration later. More importantly, the changes in the Norwegian population stock from census date to census date are the net results of net
emigration and the mortality experienced by the Norwegian population
already settled in the region. There are no mortality figures available
to take account of the number of Norwegians who died between census
dates. Despite this limitation, these figures will probably reveal in
a general way where the recurrent waves of Norwegian emigrants settled
in the United States.

By 1870 there were already more than 114,000 Norwegian emigrants
in the United States. In this early time period they predominately traveled to the North-Central region and settled there. Over one-third of
the Norwegian born stock lived in Wisconsin at this time, and Flom claims
that: "it was with Wisconsin that the chief events in early Norwegian-
American history are associated.... As all paths of the Norwegian emigrant in the early day led to Wisconsin so the threads of all subsequent
Norwegian history in America lead back to Wisconsin." [B21], p. 381.
However, the net increase of Norwegians in Minnesota was larger than that
in Wisconsin between 1850 and 1870.

During the following 20 years Minnesota is the state experiencing
by far the largest increases of Norwegian born. The Norwegian settlement
in the Dakotas also grew rapidly in this period. In 1890 almost 90 percent of the Norwegian born population in the United States lived and worked
in the North-Central region.

For the period up to 1910 the pattern of Norwegian settlement is more diversified. Of the states in the North-Central region, only North Dakota gained a substantial percentage of the total net increase. The Norwegian born population in the state of New York tripled during this 20-year span. Almost all of these lived in New York City. A third region which received a relatively large share of Norwegian emigrants after 1890 was the western one. The leading state here was Washington whose Norwegian stock in 1910 stood at almost four times its 1890 value.

This third 20-year period provided a break with the earlier pattern in yet another respect. In 1890 about one-fifth of the Norwegian born stock lived in urban areas defined as cities with 25,000 or more inhabitants. By 1910 this relative number had increased to over 40 percent of the total, and the absolute number of Norwegian born emigrants living in rural areas was actually smaller at this time compared to 20 years previously. This was, no doubt, partly due to the dying off of old rural emigrants, but it is also clear that a large share of the new Norwegian emigrants that arrived during this period chose to settle in a city. For example, the Norwegian born element in New York City more than tripled in this period, and roughly one-third of the Norwegians that traveled to Washington settled in Seattle.

How did this settlement pattern compare to that of the total foreign-born white population and the internal migration movements of the U.S. native white population? That is, was the pattern of settlement of Norwegian born emigrants very different from that of other foreign born emigrants and to what extent were these two groups replacing or complementing the movements of the native born population? To attempt to throw some light on this matter we compared the movement of these three groups into six of the states to which Norwegians typically migrated after 1870. See Table IV-4.[6]

It is reasonably clear from the figures in this table that there is no unique pattern for the six states. Throughout the 40-year period the rate of migration of all foreign born, Norwegians included, into New York was positive and quite large compared to the average foreign born base populations there. The rate of net migration of U.S. natives into this state was on the other hand negative during three of the four decades and quite small. New York may, however, be somewhat unique in the sense that most foreign born emigrants arrived at the port of New York City from abroad. Between 1870 and 1890 somewhat the same migration patterns prevailed in Illinois and Wisconsin. Net migration of native born whites were negative and they were "replaced" by foreign born white emigrants. Thus foreign born settlement in these states before 1890 was no unique Norwegian (or Scandinavian) phenomenon. After 1890 foreign born whites continued to settle in these two states while the Norwegian

[6]The figures in Table IV-4 are not strictly comparable conceptually. The figures for the native and foreign born white refer to the net migration during the decade per 1,000 of the average native and foreign born population respectively. The figures for the Norwegian born emigrants refer to net decadal changes in the population, as distinct from net migration, per 1,000 of average Norwegian born population in each state. The Norwegian figures are not standardized for mortality. Furthermore, the computed rates are sensitive to the base populations from which they are computed. We will therefore confine ourselves to a comparison of signs and rough order of magnitudes.

TABLE IV-4   136

RATES OF NET MIGRATION PER 1000 AVERAGE POPULATION OF NATIVE AND
FOREIGN BORN WHITE. NET CHANGES OF NORWEGIAN BORN PER 1000
AVERAGE NORWEGIAN BORN POPULATION

Selected U.S. States 1870-1910

	1870-1880	1880-1890	1890-1900	1900-1910
NEW YORK				
Native White	-48	-33	4	-6
Foreign Born White	209	422	368	517
Norwegians	765.8	1189.8	377	660
ILLINOIS				
Native White	-102	-62	25	-49
Foreign Born White	255	510	313	399
Norwegians	353	567	-14	93
WISCONSIN				
Native Born	-126	-82	-17	-76
Foreign Born White	252	420	218	237
Norwegians	208	284	-65	-77
NORTH DAKOTA				
Native White	1.132	733	181	322
Foreign Born White			444	453
Norwegians	1.673	1091	104	413
WASHINGTON				
Native White	676	969	214	554
Foreign Born White	947	1523	297	909
Norwegians	1392	1739	172	966
MINNESOTA				
Native Born	132	88	38	-48
Foreign Born White	598	662	253	269
Norwegians	629	472	36	4

Sources of Data: Native Born White: [B71], Table A1.19, p. 259
                Foreign Born White: [B71], Table A1.14, p. 254 and
                            [B45], Table P-4A, p. 351
            Norwegian Born: Same source as Table IV-3.

born stock decreased. Net native born migration continued to be negative. This is a reversal from the previous 20-year period.[7]

Yet a third case is provided by the state of Minnesota. All the three separate groups exhibited net increases up to 1900 and substantially so before 1890. During the first decade of the 20th century native born emigration turned negative, Norwegian born changes were insignificant, while the foreign born still traveled to Minnesota in large numbers. Finally, North Dakota and Washington provide us with cases in which all three groups exhibited roughly similar migration patterns, namely positive and high rates of migration per 1,000 of the average decadal population stocks in each group.

One should be careful before one draws sweeping conclusions from the patterns described above. But it is reasonably clear that the settlement of Norwegian born emigrants in the states to which they predominantly traveled was not a unique Norwegian phenomenon. Before 1890, the pattern of Norwegian settlement is reasonably similar to the rest of the foreign born emigrants. Thus whatever caused such a pattern cannot have been too dissimilar for the two groups. After 1890, regions of recent or new settlements attracted not only the foreign born whites, Norwegians included, but native born whites as well. Again one may speculate that a

---

[7]Net migration of Norwegian born into Illinois and Wisconsin may have been positive even after 1890. Since these were regions of early Norwegian settlements, the Norwegian born population stock was probably quite "old" in 1890 so that deaths to early settlers offset the influx of new ones after this date. The main point, namely that the movement of Norwegian born resembled much more that of the native white population than that of the total foreign born, is not altered by such a consideration.

set of opportunities that appealed to all three groups was in operation.
If such a general argument has any merit, this cannot have been the
case in the "older" regions in the North-Central region, particularly
Illinois and Wisconsin. That is to say, in these places employment opportunities after 1890 must have been such that these states were able
to attract foreign born whites, but not Norwegians and the U.S. born.

IV-4. Sex and Age Distribution of Norwegian
Overseas Emigrants

After 1866 there is information on the sex and age distribution
of Norwegians who departed for overseas destinations. Since we view the
migration process as the movement of labor between regions, we are mainly
interested in the relative number of emigrants in the prime working ages
here defined to be migrants between the ages of 15 to 49. The figures
in Table IV-5 refer to the average relative number in each age and sex
category during the long swing periods we marked off in aggregate overseas emigration.

Throughout the period a predominant number of migrants were between
15 and 49 years of age. Furthermore, the relative share of this age
group in the total migration stream increases over time. Before 1877
almost two-thirds of the migrants were in the prime working ages. During
the third long swing this figure stood at almost 90 percent of the total.
If we disaggregate and compare the age-groups 15 to 29 and 30 to 49 years
of age, we see that this trend is entirely due to the rapidly rising

TABLE IV-5

RELATIVE NUMBERS OF NORWEGIAN EMIGRANTS IN SELECTED AGE AND SEX GROUPS
Long Swing Averages 1866-1936

	1866–1877	1877–1897	1897–1918	1918–1936
Males 0–14	15.66	10.54	5.95	5.52
Males 15–29	23.44	33.90	46.99	40.12
Males 30–49	13.21	10.63	9.25	14.96
Males 15–49	36.65	44.53	56.24	55.08
Females 0–14	14.26	10.48	5.62	5.40
Females 15–29	16.87	22.15	24.90	20.39
Females 30–49	9.99	7.57	6.53	9.51
Females 15–49	26.87	29.72	31.43	29.90
All Persons above 50	6.56	4.75	0.75	4.09
Total	100.00	100.00	100.00	100.00

Source of Data: For the period 1866-1918: [B19], Norway, Table II, pp. 748-50.
For the period 1918-1916: [G23], Table 100, pp. 204-05.

share of the younger of the two groups. The upward trend among the males between 15 and 29 is especially noticeable. The relative share of this group more than doubled between the first and the third period. During the long swing which included World War I, almost fifty percent of the total number of migrants were males in this age category.

The relative share of female emigrants in prime working ages changed less than the corresponding share of male emigrants. As a percent of total migration it rose from 26 to a little over 36 percent. Thus the ratio of male to female emigrants between the ages of 15 and 49 rose over the period. Exactly how many of the females in this age group that merely emigrated with their husbands rather than in pursuit of jobs is hard to say. Of all the female emigrants above 15 that emigrated between 1890 and 1920, a little over one-fifth were married. After 1920 this number increased somewhat. It is therefore fair to conclude that Norwegian overseas migrants increasingly consisted of young males below 30 years of age or presumably the most mobile part of the Norwegian labor force. What were the occupations of these migrants? To that we now briefly turn.

IV-5. Occupational Distributions of Norwegian Migrants

5.1. The Occupations of Emigrants in Norway Before Leaving

The occupations of Norwegian male emigrants were recorded starting in the 1870's, while similar tabulations for female migrants started as late as 1903. In 1919 an entirely new classification code was adopted.

We will therefore confine ourselves to a brief description of the occupations of male Norwegian emigrants between 1876 and 1915. The relative distribution of these occupations is set forth as averages for two subperiods in Table IV-6.

From the figures in this table we see that Norwegian farmers that owned land never constituted a large relative share of the Norwegian emigration stream. Rather it was the landless farmers and laborers that made up by far the largest group before 1915; over 60 percent during the very heavy emigration wave between the 1870's and the middle 1890's, and almost 50 percent thereafter. Comprehensive data on the rate of emigration of such unskilled rural laborers per 1,000 of average total employment in these occupational groups is hard to compute because of differences in classifications. But the occupational-specific emigration rates in these groups must have been quite high. For example, during the period 1896-1915 almost 36 out of every 1,000 laborers employed in agriculture on the average emigrated while only between one and two out of every 1,000 farmers who owned land did so.

Two other occupational groups emigrated in relatively large numbers, both considerably more skilled than the first one. I refer to the emigrants who were employed in handicrafts (group 7) and water transport (group 10) before leaving. The relative shares of these two groups exhibited an upward trend and together accounted for approximately 30 percent of total male emigrants above 15 between the 1890's and 1915. Furthermore, the occupational-specific emigration rates for these groups were relatively high. Around 11 per 1,000 of average employment in handicrafts

TABLE IV-6   142

OCCUPATIONS OF NORWEGIAN MALE EMIGRANTS 15 YEARS AND OVER. 1876-1915

A: Per Cent of Total Male Emigrants
B: Per 1000 of Average Domestic Employment in Selected Groups

	1876 - 1895		1896 - 1915	
	A	B	A	B
(1) Farmers, Cotters with Land	5.47	3.06	2.97	1.53
(2) Fishermen	0.80	0.90	4.94	
GROUP I = 1+2	6.27		7.92	
(3) Family Labor Agricultural	6.95	12.78	5.81	6.02
(4) Other Labor Agricultural			20.22	35.60
(5) Daily Labor, Labor Unspecified Domestic Servants	53.72		20.69	
GROUP II = 3+4+5	60.67		46.72	
(6) Mining, Manufacturing	1.63	3.05	5.63	7.08
(7) Handicrafts	11.37	10.40	13.31	12.58
(8) Small Industries and Others	0.38	2.00	2.58	7.05
GROUP III = 6+7+8	13.38		21.52	
(9) Commerce, Land Transport	2.99	7.10	5.35	6.48
(10) Water Transport	11.40	28.95	16.35	30.28
(11) Other Transport	0.18	1.25	0.28	4.68
GROUP IV = 9+10+11	14.57		21.97	
OTHER	5.10		1.87	
TOTAL	100.00		100.00	

Sources of Data: Computed from [G13], Table V, pp. 114-15.

and approximately 30 per 1,000 in water transport. The last figure is almost as high as that found for agricultural laborers.

These three groups have, despite considerable differences in skill mix, one thing in common. During the period in question they must all have been experiencing som technological unemployment. The developments in the Norwegian economy that were mainly responsible for this were briefly alluded to in Chapter II. Major transformations occurred in Norwegian agriculture and shipping after the 1870's consisting of radical changes in technology. Old labor intensive production techniques were replaced by much more capital intensive ones. This must have, at least in the short run, caused stagnant aggregate demand for labor in these industries. It is hard to quantify exactly how important such "push" factors were in determining, perhaps "selecting", which occupational groups emigrated. To do that we have to specify the production function in each industry and exactly how it changed during this period. We doubt that this is possible, and in any event it is beyond the scope of this investigation.

In the final analysis, the question of "who leaves" may well be simultaneously determined by the excess demand for occupational skills in the region of arrival in addition to excess supply considerations in the area of departure. We will therefore consider the occupations of Norwegian born emigrants in the U.S. next.

5.2. Occupations of the Norwegian Born Emigrants in the U.S.

If the occupational distribution of Norwegian born emigrants (for example of a given skill) differs from their occupations in the region of departure but is very similar to the occupational distribution of domestic workers of comparable skills in the region to which they migrate, one can say that the occupational distribution was determined by employment opportunities in the last region. If, on the other hand, the distribution is very much like the one exhibited in the region of the departure, but differs substantially from that of the gainfully employed U.S. born, one may claim their "old" occupations largely determine the nature of their work also in their new country.

Finally, if their occupational distribution in the U.S. is very similar to both their old occupations and the total U.S., one is tempted to say that employment opportunities in the U.S. not only determined the occupational distribution in the region of arrival, but also "selects" who leaves Norway.

The U.S. census record of the occupations of the foreign born begins with 1870 according to a census monograph by Hutchinson [B29]. Unfortunately, in the censuses of 1870, 1880 and 1890 Norwegians are listed together with Danes and Swedes, so that the census of 1900 is the first to reveal typical occupations of Norwegian born emigrants separately. The next U.S. census to list occupations of foreign born by nation of birth is the one taken in 1950. We are therefore limited to one data point in the comparison to follow. The figures in Table IV-7 refer to the occupational distributions of Norwegian born, foreign born white and native born white breadwinners ten years of age and over.[8]

---

[8]According to the U.S. Immigration Commission, "the term breadwinner is used to include everyone who is engaged in any gainful occupation." [G29], p. 777.

TABLE IV-7   145

RELATIVE OCCUPATIONAL DISTRIBUTION BY MAJOR OCCUPATIONAL GROUP AND SEX: 1900

Norwegian Born Immigrants, Foreign Born White Workers and
Native Born White Workers

	MALES			FEMALES		
	Norwegian Born	Foreign Born	Native Born	Norwegian Born	Foreign Born	Native Born
(1) Agricultural Pursuits	49.8	21.2	41.8	13.8	4.7	11.2
Agricultural Laborers	11.5					
Farmers, planters	37.0					
Other group (1)	1.3					
(2) Professional Service	1.8	2.4	4.2	2.6	3.0	12.5
(3) Domestic and Personal Service	12.8	20.2	11.7	64.0	53.1	30.3
Laborers (not specified)	9.5					
All others in group (3)	3.3					
(4) Trade and Transportation	12.5	17.5	19.8	4.2	7.2	14.0
(5) Manufacturing and Mechanical Pursuits	23.2	38.8	22.5	15.4	32.0	32.0
Building Trades	7.9					
Rest of group (5)	15.3					
All Occupations	100.0	100.0	100.0	100.0	100.0	100.0

Sources of Data: Norwegian Born Immigrants: [G28]; Males: Table 117, p. 177,
                          Females: Table Ib, pp. 240-45.

                 Foreign Born and Native Born White: Computed from [B29],
                          Table 31, p. 159.

If we confine ourselves to the occupational distribution of Norwegian born males for the moment, we see that over 60 percent belonged to the two groups: Agricultural Pursuits (group 1), and Domestic and Personal Service (group 3). Referring back to Table IV-6 for a moment, this figure is quite comparable to the average relative number of farmers and laborers that emigrated from Norway between 1876 and 1895. (The combined percentages of group I and group II in Table IV-6 add up to 67.) The difference is that while the occupation of laborer dominated among the emigrants, that of farmer is the predominant occupation among Norwegian born immigrants. Where it comes to the two categoreis Trade and Transportation and Manufacturing and Mechanical Pursuits (groups (4) and (5) in Table IV-7) they are similar to the relative numbers of emigrants that had these occupations when they left Norway. (See groups III and IV in Table IV-6.) This alone would indicate that the occupational distributions of Norwegian emigrants were largely determined by their professions in the "old country".

However, before we jump to such a conclusion we should note the similar occupational distributions of the Norwegian born and the native born whites in Table IV-7. That is, the distribution of Norwegians in the U.S. is similar to both their old occupations and that in the total U.S. Does this mean that the true explanation, instead of the one proposed immediately above, is that employment opportunities in the U.S. not only determined the occupational distribution in the region of arrival, but also "selected" which type of labor left Norway?

To make more definite statements we would need data on the occupational distribution of the two groups by subregions or states. That is, we would like to compare the occupational distribution of Norwegian born emigrants in the states where they typically settled with the occupational distribution of native born whites in these states. For example, in 1900 more than one-third of the Norwegian born farmers were located in the state of Minnesota and more than one-fifth in the state of Wisconsin, and over 95 percent in the North-Central region. [G28], Table 118, pp. 178-79. This was a region, to be sure, in which the percentage of total labor force in agriculture was generally above the U.S. average.[9] But to make a more refined comparison we would need data on the percentages of Norwegian born and native born whites in agriculture in these states. Such figures, to the best of our knowledge, do not exist.

It is also unfortunate that the occupational figures are not available separately for Norwegians at an earlier date. We have already observed that the states where the overwhelming number of Norwegian farmers lived in 1900 were largely occupied by Norwegian emigrants some time before this date. We doubt that most of the Norwegian born emigrants were able and could afford to settle as farmers immediately upon arrival. It is more likely that a large number participated in the early settlement period as agricultural laborers or as laborers in the rapidly growing railroad and lumber industries, or in other occupations. Only after a while had they saved enough to get their own farms.

---

[9]If the U.S. average is set equal to 100, the percent of the total labor force in agriculture relative to that of the U.S. was as follows in 1900: Wisconsin 105, Minnesota 112, Iowa 132, North and South Dakota 166. Source: [B41], Table A.2.5, p. 83.

In the states further east with a Norwegian born population of some importance, namely Illinois and New York, the group Manufacturing and Mechanical Pursuits was the most important one, containing around 50 percent of the Norwegian born male breadwinners living there. Within this group, the building trades were the most important. In the state of New York alone the number of Norwegian boatmen and sailors constituted 16.8 percent of the total number of Norwegian male breadwinners. The percent of the total labor force in Transportation in New York in 1900 was 8.2. (See Kuznets ibid., Table A.2.7, p. 86.) Thus to the extent that these two figures are comparable, they would tend to show that Norwegian emigrant sailors "selected" to settle in New York rather than the other way around.

The point of presenting these scattered figures for subregions and states within the U.S. is only to stress that we feel that sweeping conclusions from the aggregate data in Table IV-7 are unwarranted. The occupational distributions of Norwegian born in subregions were most likely very different from the aggregate distribution, and the distributions of Norwegians in each region may also have been different from that of the native born white, at least in the East. They also give some indication that the Norwegian emigrants that we characterized as skilled, notably labor employed in handicrafts and shipping, rather than changing their occupations traveled to areas where there was excess demand for their particular skills. The sailors settled in New York, at Lake Michigan and on the West Coast, and so on.

As far as the unskilled (agricultural) laborer is concerned, addi-

tional forces may have been at work. Norwegian emigrants in this category may have been less mobile than the total of U.S. unskilled workers
due to the existence of ethnic ties leading to concentrated settlements
in the North-Central region. They may also have depended to some extent
on arrangements made by relatives or friends previous to arrival. The
distribution of unskilled Norwegians may also have depended to a considerable extent on other contractoral and institutional arrangements,
at least in the earlier period. According to a recent study by Erickson:
"The combination of banker, boardinghouse keeper, and labor agent, which
Americans have associated with the southern European emigration, partly
because the first government investigations were not made until the 1900
decade, was to be found in Chicago both before and after the great fire.
No fewer than eleven labor agencies dealing in Scandinavian labor adver-
tised in the newspapers during this period.... Among them was the Scandinavian Emigrant Agency which handled Guion Line passengers, and after 1871,
Cunard Line passengers as well.... These labor bureaus dealt primarily
in railroad labor. Whereas in the fifties, the Illinois Central had had
to send its agent to New York City to find emigrant labor, the flood of
Scandinavian emigrants into Chicago after the war transformed Chicago into
the center of railway employment in the country." [B17], pp. 90-91.

Given their skills, and aside from ethnic and institutional arrangements, from an economic point of view it was perfectly rational for Norwegian emigrants with largely an agricultural background to migrate to the
North-Central and later to the Western regions. If the agricultural service
income per worker in the U.S. is set equal to 100, the relative figures in

1880 and 1900 respectively were as follows: East-North Central 131 and
123, West-North Central 102 and 156, and Pacific 174 and 173. [B41],
Table 4.3 B, p. 152.[10] Presumably such figures reflect to a certain
extent the differences in regional excess demands for labor of this
particular skill. The settlement pattern of Norwegians is consistent
with such differences, and it is quite likely that regional wage-dif-
ferentials for unskilled (agricultural) labor played a role, in addition to the ones we have sketched above, in determining the regional
distribution of Norwegian born emigrants.

IV-6. Return Migration from the U. S. to Norway

As was mentioned briefly in Chapter II, Norwegian immigration
statistics before World War II are not as comprehensive as one would
wish. Yearly records of Norwegian emigrants that returned from the U.S.
do not exist. We have to rely upon information on returned emigrants
given in the Norwegian Censuses of 1910 and 1920. According to the figures contained therein, return migration of the Norwegian born was
negligible before 1895 and relatively small even after that. If we compute return migration from the U.S. as a percent of overseas migration
to that country, the figures for the periods 1876-95 and 1896-1920 were

---

[10]The figures on agricultural service income per worker in typically "Norwegian" states relative to the U.S. average (=100) were as
follows for the dates 1880 and 1900: Illinois 151 and 148, Wisconsin
126 and 117, Minnesota 121 and 132, Iowa 141 and 179, North Dakota 61
and 194, Washington 117 and 148, Oregon 162 and 150. Kuznets, ibid.,
Table A.4.6, p. 190.

1.26 and 14.38 respectively.[11] The first figure is probably too low
since it is based on information from persons still living in 1910.
Clearly some of the return migrants may simply have died before this
date. The latter figure is more accurate, and must still be considered quite low compared to other groups of migrants. And if we exclude
the decade between 1910 and 1920, which may be considered exceptional
due to World War I, the return figure for the 15 years between 1895
and 1910 is below 7 as a percent of the number of emigrants.

Kuznets and Rubin provide some information on the ratio of departures to arrivals of all alien passengers. During the two subperiods
1876-1895 and 1896-1920 departures as a percent of arrivals were 25.5
and 48.5 respectively.[12] Thus Norwegian return migration was very much
below that of all aliens. Unfortunatley there is no data on the departures of aliens by country of birth. The only official U.S. figures
refer to emigration of aliens by country of future residence and start
as late as 1908. For the period 1908 to 1919, the number of emigrants
that listed their future residence as Norway coincides well with the
1920 Norwegian census figure on Norwegian born that returned from the
U.S. in the same period.

In concluding, I think it is fair to say that, even though the

---

[11]The absolute numbers of returned Norwegian born emigrants from
the U.S. in each time period was taken from [G13], p. 75 and [B3],
Table 106, p. 182, respectively.

[12]These two ratios were computed from Kuznets and Rubin [B40],
Table B-1, pp. 95-6. The data on departures of all alien passengers
may be biased since there is no direct information on the departures of
aliens as distinct from U.S. citizens. See ibid., p. 57.

statistics are not very comprehensive, relatively few Norwegians that emigrated to the U.S. returned before World War I. If we therefore in the following chapter limit the analysis of Norwegian gross out-migration (to the U.S.) to the period before 1914, something that may be desirable for other reasons as well, the lack of yearly figures on returning emigrants may not be so serious.

CHAPTER V

ECONOMIC MODELS OF NORWEGIAN EMIGRATION

TO THE UNITED STATES

> "The decision to emigrate may obviously
> result from a number of motives, which
> may differ in each individual case.
> But, generally speaking, among these
> motives an economic consideration, the
> desire to become better off, has been
> predominant."
>
> J. Isaac.
> Economics of Migration.
> Oxford: Oxford Univ. Press, 1947, p.23.

V-1. Introduction

The emigration of Norwegians to the United States is an important
example of a substantial interregional transfer of population. Between
the U. S. Civil War and World War I, Norway lost well over 40 percent of
her natural increase, the highest national per capita figure during this
time period save Ireland. Yet there is little in Norway's religious-
political-social history of the time period to account for such heavy
out-migration. See for example [B61]. It would therefore seem interesting to attempt to explain this emigration movement in terms of economic
and demographic factors. Thus the basic analytical premise is to view
historical emigration as a transfer of labor responding to relative economic opportunities.

It is a well-known fact of economic development that accelerated economic growth and industrialization have been associated with a transfer of labor from rural-based traditional agriculture to urban-oriented modern industry. The breaking up of the pre-industrial economy in Norway occurred simultaneously with the opening up of the international economy encompassing the Atlantic economic community. Thus Norwegian internal and external labor mobility increased at the same time, as has been alluded to several times in previous chapters. However, most of the economic literature on historical migration to the New World fails to take this explicitly into account. The question is rarely asked to what extent a job in the emerging modern sector in the native country was an alternative to working overseas, at least in the short run.

The objective of this chapter is twofold. First, I shall formulate an economic behavioral model of historical emigration which, in my opinion, represents a realistic modification and extension of the simple unemployment approach commonly found in the existing literature [B32], [B69], [A20], [A43]. It does so by recognizing the dual nature of the country of departure at the time of movement and by introducing the returns to emigration and prior demographic events as possible determinants of the overseas labor transfer process.

Secondly, I will test how well such a model is able to predict yearly Norwegian emigration to the U.S. The results obtained differ from much of the previous work done on several specific points regarding for example the importance of "push" versus "pull" effects, and the causes of the prominent long swings in historical emigration, as will be discussed in some detail below.

In the final section I review critically the analytical content of the unemployment models of Jerome [B32], D. S. Thomas [B69], Kelley [A20], and Wilkinson [A43]. Furthermore, it is argued that some of the conclusions drawn in these studies are open to criticism on methodological-statistical grounds. Finally, I show that the above theories provide incomplete explanations of the overseas emigration of Norwegians to the U.S over the very period within which these models have generally been applied.

V-2. The Model

2.1. The Individual Propensity to Migrate

Consider the individual decision to migrate. In deciding whether or not to migrate, an individual will assess the expected returns to moving. My contention is that, _ceteris paribus_, an individual worker will move to another region or country where his permanent income position can be improved. If he emigrates, he may expect a stream of earnings in the country of arrival Y_{A1}^e, Y_{A2}^e,....Y_{An}^e over periods 1, 2 ... n respectively. If he does not emigrate, his alternative is a stream of expected earnings in the country of origin Y_{01}, Y_{02},....Y_{0n}. The net return to emigration would be the difference of the present values of the sum over periods 1 to n. In deciding whether or not to move, then, the individual compares the present value of emigrating

$$(2.1.1) \qquad PV_A = \sum_{j=1}^{n} \frac{Y_{Aj}^e}{(1+rA)^j}$$

to the long run opportunity cost of moving

$$(2.1.2) \qquad PV_O = \sum_{j=1}^{n} \frac{Y_{Oj}^e}{(1+r0)^j}$$

where rA and r0 are discount rates assumed for simplicity to be the
same in each period. If it can be assumed, furthermore, that rA is
approximately equal to r0 equal to r, the present value of the net
expected future benefits of migrating from O to A is

$$(2.1.3) \qquad PY^e = PV_A - PV_O = \sum_{j=1}^{n} \frac{Y_{Aj}^e - Y_{Oj}^e}{(1+r)^j}$$

Earnings in this discussion in principle include nonpecuniary, or psychic,
as well as pecuniary components. The possible influence of nonpecuniary
factors on emigration will be made explicit below. At this point one
may think of it as included in Y_{Aj}^e and Y_{Oj}^e.

Future net expected earnings cannot be measured directly. In order
to arrive at hypotheses that can be tested empirically, one must attempt
to specify how such expectations are formed in terms of the actual earning differences that prevailed at the time of emigration. It seems plausible to hypothesize that expectations about future earnings are a function of those that could be observed at the time of emigration, time t,
and the years prior to year t. Thus

$$(2.1.4) \qquad PY_t^e = f(Y_t, Y_{t-1}, Y_{t-2}, Y_{t-3}, \ldots)$$

where Y_t refers to the actual observable earnings difference between A
and O in year t and so on. Assuming a linear form of this function we
have

$$(2.1.5) \quad PY_t^e = \alpha_o Y_t + \alpha_1 Y_{t-1} + \alpha_2 Y_{t-2} + \alpha_3 Y_{t-3} \cdots$$

$$= \sum_{i=0}^{T} \alpha_i Y_{t-i} \qquad i = 0, 1, \ldots T$$

There are now numerous possibilities as to the exact specification of the individual migrant's expectation function. However, I feel that there are no strong theoretical reasons that would lead to a more exact a priori specification of (2.1.5). Rather, I will return to this point in the section below where I discuss the complete explanatory equation to be tested empirically.

Having decided on the basis of present and past earning differences that conditions are favorable to emigration from O to A, the individual emigrant must decide exactly when to move. Presumable, the migrant will attempt to minimize the cost of moving, and one must therefore attempt to identify the elements of costs involved in transferring from region O to region A. One such obvious element includes the out-of-pocket expenses of travel, namely the increase in expenditure for food, lodging, transportation, etc., necessitated by migration. A second major factor is the short-run opportunity cost, i.e., the earnings foregone while traveling and searching for a new job.[1] Thus it is suggested that

$$(2.1.6) \quad TC_t = g(TRC_t, SOC_t)$$

where TC refers to the total transfer costs, TRC is traveling costs, and SOC refers to the short-run opportunity cost of movement.

---

[1] This should be distinguished from what was called the long-run opportunity cost of moving above, namely PV_o.

TRC will partly be a function of distance traveled and the means of transportation and as such needs little further specification. I argue, furthermore, that the short-run opportunity cost of movement will be related to the probabilities of obtaining jobs in both regions. Thus

$$(2.1.7) \qquad SOC_t = g_1(P_{At}; P_{Ot})$$

where P_{At} and P_{Ot} refer to such job probabilities in regions A and O respectively.

A considerable earnings premium in country A is of little consequence to a prospective emigrant if his chances of actually securing a job there in year t is very low. One important question is, then, how long it takes the migrant to get a job in the region of arrival. I hypothesize that this in turn will be a function of the rate of unemployment there, U_{At}. A booming labor market in A would shorten the period it takes the migrant to get a job in his new country, and he would thus minimize foregone earnings while searching for a job by timing his arrival in A accordingly. In other words,

$$(2.1.8) \qquad P_{At} = g_2(U_{At})$$

If the worker is already unemployed in O at time t, he would presumably forego no earnings while traveling. Or, alternatively, the potential migrant might be a marginal farm worker not subject to unemployment before moving.[2] However, if O consists of two distinct economic regions,

---

[2] One reason for this is the existence of traditional cropsharing activities and the so-called "extended family" system which largely negates the impact of unemployment in the traditional sector.

an urban industrializing sector uO in addition to a rural sector rO, employment probabilities in uO may enter as an argument. Given P_{At}, the probability of getting a job in uO at time t, P_{uOt}, should affect the short-run opportunity costs of emigrating to A. If, from the point of view of a worker in rO, P_{uOt} is low, his propensity to emigrate to A in year t should be higher, _ceteris paribus_. Similarly, the worker already in uO will minimize lost income of emigrating to A by leaving when he becomes unemployed in the urban domestic economy. I thus postulate that

$$(2.1.9) \quad P_{uOt} = g_3(U_{uOt})$$

where U_{uOt} is the rate of unemployment in uO. Using (2.1.8) and (2.1.9) and substituting into (2.1.7) we have

$$(2.1.10) \quad SOC_t = g_4(U_{At}, U_{uOt})$$

One may speculate on the relative sensitivity of labor emigration to changes in the unemployment rates of the source and of the receiving countries. As specified in (2.1.10), the hypothesis regarding "pull" versus "push" effects will be confined to a consideration of the relative impact of unemployment variations in the country of arrival and the urban sector in the country of origin upon the exact timing of emigration.[3]

---

[3]In principle, one may conceive of unemployment as affecting the transfer of labor from one country to another in two ways. First, short run fluctuations in the unemployment rates affect the timing of departure of a given long-term flow as was postulated above. Secondly, spatial differences in the long-run or mean unemployment rates may affect the long-term level of emigration through their impact on the respective expected

Using (2.1.10) and (2.1.6) we have that

(2.1.11) $TC_t = g(TRC_t; U_{At}, U_{uOt})$.

According to (2.1.5) and (2.1.11) it is argued that emigration of the kth individual from O to A at time t, kM_t, can be expressed by

$$(2.1.12) \quad kM_t = f(\sum_{i=o}^{T} \alpha i Y_{t-i}); g(TRC_t; U_{At}, U_{uOt})$$

$$i = 0,1\ldots T$$

2.2. Determinants of Aggregate Emigration

I will now attempt to specify the relationship describing the determinants of aggregate labor emigration from O to A . Given the existing opportunities for emigration, and given the individual responses to these opportunities, it is hypothesized that the volume of aggregate emigration will be a function of the supply of potential emigrants in O, i.e., the relative number of people in the very mobile ages where workers typically migrate. Several earlier writers on historical overseas emigration have entertained somewhat similar "demographic hypotheses". For instance, Spengler states that: "Whilst absolute natural increase increased very little in Europe between 1820 and the First World War, it fluctuated considerably, producing corresponding fluctuations in accessions to the labor force fifteen or more years later and apparently oc-

---

income streams in the two regions. Todaro, in a recent article on internal migration in underdeveloped countries, stresses the latter aspect. See [A38], pp. 139-142. Unfortunately, the available historical data is not sufficiently refined to enable us to test the latter hypothesis empirically.

casioning fluctuations in the volume of emigration about twenty-five years later." [B63], p. 45. However, no further details are given.

I will argue that the relevant demographic factor to focus on is the pool of mobile persons or potential emigrants. This pool, in turn, is a function of prior demographic events including previous emigration. That is to say, the number of young persons, for example of age x, living in O at time t is not only a function of the size of the birth cohort at time t-x and its survival ratio up to time t, it is in addition a function of the number of people in this birth cohort that have already left O prior to year t. Thus it is argued that prior emigration may influence emigration in year t, via the size of pool of potential emigrants, in two ways. If emigration in year t-x was comparatively heavy, the size of the birth cohort in that year is likely to have been relatively small. Secondly, as has already been mentioned, the larger the number of emigrants from a given birth cohort in the time period between t-x and t, the smaller the pool of potential emigrants at time t. I will refer to this effect as the cohort effect, CO_t, in the following sections.

Prior emigration may conceivably influence aggregate migration in year t in yet another way, namely via the stock of people born in O that now live and work in A. This may be so for several reasons. First of all, friends and relatives already in A can provide information on working and living conditions there.[4] They may send tickets or passage fares

---

[4]In one earlier study of migration it is argued that the magnitude of information is, indeed, a key determinant of geographical labor mobility. See Nelson [A29]. Unfortunately, the difficulties involved in measuring information renders his empirical results inconclusive at best.

back to their "old country". And, finally, such a stock may affect the non-pecuniary or psychic aspects of overseas emigration.

Aside from such general considerations, more empirical information is clearly needed on each specific point before one can attempt to specify exactly how prior emigration will influence emigration of labor in year t. As will be seen below, empirical data regarding these aspects is excessively scarce.

Aggregating over all individual emigrants in prime working ages the postulated macro-relationship may be stated as follows:

$$(2.2.1) \quad M_t = F(\sum_{i=0}^{T} \alpha i Y_{t-i}, \; CO_t, \; SPM_t); \; G(TRC_t, \; U_{At}, \; U_{uOt})$$

where $M_t = \sum_k kM_t \quad k = 1, 2.... \text{ emigrants}$

and Y, TRC, and the U's are for notational convenience redefined to represent aggregates. Thus I hypothesize that the aggregate long-term level of emigration from O to A is a function of past income differences, a pool of potential emigrants in O, and the stock of prior emigrants from O to A. The timing of departure of such a long term flow will depend on the short-run costs of moving.

Several assumptions regarding individual behaviour is implied by the above aggregation procedure. Consider for example the way expectations regarding future benefits are formed. First, one might suppose that every individual emigrant, every component of the aggregate volume of emigration in any year t possesses a reaction of the same type, i.e., that the relationship postulated in (2.1.5) above holds good for every individual. A second possibility is that each individual responds dif-

ferently to past observable earning differences so that when the aggregation is performed the result is a distributed lag or moving average
structure for the aggregate reaction. Even though the latter interpretation may seem to be the most plausible a priori, I will find myself
unable to distinguish between them in the empirical tests of this relationship that I now proceed to discuss.

V-3. The Empirical Tests

3.1. The Data Used

Time series data are used to estimate a modified version of equation (2.2.1), derived at the end of the preceding section. The following
available empirical measures of the specified variables are used.

3.1.1. M_t, the Emigration Rate.

As the dependent variable I use the rate of Norwegian emigrants to
the United States. Since the focus is on the historical emigration of
labor, only persons in the prime working ages are included. In this way
it is hoped that many of the dependents in the emigration stream will be
weeded out. Indeed, the basic hypotheses set forth above makes sense
a priori only when applied to this age-group rather than the total number of emigrants each year. Furthermore, I standardize for the size of
the total Norwegian population in prime working ages by expressing the
dependent variable as a rate of emigration per thousand of mean Norwegian
population in this age group.

$$M_t = \frac{nMxt}{nNPxt} \cdot 1000$$

where nMxt = the absolute number of emigrants from Norway to the
U.S. between the ages x and x+n in year t.

        nNPxt = the average Norwegian population between the ages x
and x+n in year t

x = 15 and n = 30 unless otherwise specified.[5]

3.1.2. PY_t, the Permanent Income Difference.

Real GNP per member of labor force in the U.S. and Norway was

chosen as the empirical proxy for the difference in the level of living

between the two countries. It is hypothesized that the notion of perma-

nent income differences refers to the actual observable average of the

five previous years. This implicitly assumes that migrants believe that

the observable (past) difference will remain roughly constant in the

future. These years are, furthermore, given equal weights.[6]

---

[5]As will be seen below, I will proceed to divide the total number
of emigrants between the ages of 15 and 44 into subgroups according to
their age and sex in order to test the validity of the model at a more
disaggregated level.

[6]The hypothesis regarding permanent income suggested here is a
special case of the more general distributed lag hypothesis

$$(3.1.1) \quad PY_t^e = \sum_{i=o}^{1-1} \alpha i Y_{t-i} + \alpha 1 \sum_{m=o}^{\infty} \beta^m Y_{t-(1+m)}$$

where $0 \leq \beta < 1$, $m \geq 0$.

If $k \neq 0$, $\beta = 0$, the longest lag in (3.1.1) is the kth. Set k = 6 and
give αi, i = 1...5, equal weights, then we have the hypothesis that will
be tested empirically. If, on the other hand, k = 0 and $\alpha \beta < 1$, we get a
distributed lag hypothesis specifying geometrically declining weights as
we move back in time. However, since our objective is merely to see if a
plausible proxy of long run gain is significantly associated with emigration, and given the crudeness of the yearly GNP data, I will limit myself
to a moving average hypothesis.

From a logical point of view, one should attempt to make a check
for possible income distribution differences between the two countries.
Unfortunately, comprehensive data on this score is largely unavailable.[7]
Further, one would have liked to differentiate between labor income differences and property income differences and compare per worker non-
property income in the two countries instead of G.N.P. per worker. Data
on this score is unavailable in Norway before 1910. I am therefore
forced to compare average productivity of labor whereas marginal productivity comparisons might have been preferable.[8]

There are, in addition, some well-known index number problems in
international comparisons of real incomes. Using figures in constant
prices, the Norwegian G.N.P. was converted into dollar equivalents by
applying the market exchange rate. One difficulty with this conversion
is, of course, that such an exchange rate may only reflect the prices of
internationally traded goods and services. A second difficulty is that
a Norwegian krone at the time may not have represented a command over
the same representative basket of goods and services as its equivalent
(corrected for changes in price levels with reference to a base year) in

---

[7]To be sure, some information is available for the 19th century.
However, for the U.S. before 1909, Denison comments that: "We return,
then, to the key question whether the data can support any analysis or
conclusion with respect to the distribution of income by type. My impression is, obviously, that they cannot." [B13], p. 403. More recent
studies on the U.S. are either limited to the high-income groups [A36]
or to bench mark figures on the distribution of wealth [B23]. Soltow's
study on Norway refers only to a few cities for the period in question.
See [B62a].

[8]For an attempt to use bench mark wage figures in the two countries to assess the plausability of the G.N.P. comparisons, see Appendix B where the data used is discussed in more detail.

U.S. dollars could purchase at the time in the U.S.A. To assess how serious such problems are in our case is probably impossible given the data available, and it is certainly beyond the scope of the study. It may, instead, be reasonable to assume that most potential Norwegian emigrants did not possess any detailed information on prices and costs of living in the U.S., but rather that they simply used the exchange rate in their comparisons, as I did.

Finally, there is the question of non-pecuniary returns. Cursory examination of things like hours of work, working conditions generally, provision of public goods and services like education and other welfare services does not point to any great differences between the two countries at the time. Other factors like social status, etc., are impossible to quantify altogether. It will therefore be assumed that non-pecuniary returns can be treated as a constant for the purposes of the empirical tests. Thus

$$PY_t = \sum_{i=t-1}^{t-6} \frac{G.N.P._i^{US}}{L} \Big/ 5 - \sum_{i=t-1}^{t-6} \frac{G.N.P._i^{N}}{L} \Big/ 5$$

where $G.N.P./L$ = real Gross National Product per
member of labor force

U.S. and N refer to U.S.A. and Norway respectively
and the Norwegian figures are expressed in dollar
equivalents.

3.1.3. CO_t, the Cohort Effect.

As a proxy for such a variable I propose to use the relative number of Norwegians in the age-group 20 to 29 years of age living in Norway in year t-1. The reason for chosing this particular age-group will become clear when I discuss the empirical findings below and compare them with earlier studies.

$$CO_t = \frac{mNPyt-1}{nNPxt-1} \cdot 1000$$

where

$mNPyt-1$ = the absolute number of persons between ages y and y+m living in Norway in year t-1

$nNPxt-1$ = the absolute number of persons between ages x and x+n living in Norway in year t-1

y = 20 and m = 10,

x = 15 and n = 30.

3.1.4. UAt = UUSt. Empirical Proxy : EUSt.

Direct information on unemployment variations is unavailable for the U.S. before 1890. As an empirical proxy for job availabilities I chose Frickey's index on production for trade and transportation, as percent deviations from a fitted trend. There are several reasons for this choice. First, the zero order correlation coefficient between this series and Lebergott's estimates of unemployment for part of the period is high. Between 1890 and 1914 the correlation coefficient equals -0.85 on a yearly basis.[9] Secondly, railroad activity possesses a heavy weight in the index, and at least one prominent student of U.S. economic development in the 19th century assigns a key role to railroad development as an indicator of job availabilities in the westward expansion in general,

---

[9]For a detailed comparison of these two series, see Appendix B.

and in Western agriculture in particular.[10]

3.1.5. UUOt = UNt

Aggregate unemployment figures for Norway are now available
starting in 1865. I therefore use these estimates since production
indexes are unavailable before 1909. It is important to remember, then,
that the measure of variations in employment opportunities in the U.S.
refers to employment (or output relative to trend), while the Norwegian proxy is unemployment. I return to this point when I discuss the
empirical results.

3.1.6. TRCt, the Direct Cost of Travel.

On a second main element in the short run cost of moving, namely
the cost of travel itself, TRCt, there is no yearly information before
World War I. However, during the period I intend to analyze, there were
no major technical innovations in the means of transportation. More importantly from our point of view, there appears to have been very little
secular change in the price of the ticket. By the early 1870's almost
all the passenger travel was by steamship, which meant a substantial

---

[10]Fishlow states that: "..., the mechanism that seems to have
operated in the 1850's may be described, in equally simplified terms, as
follows. The increased opportunities for employment in the West associated with railroad construction, actual and anticipated, promoted a considerable migration into the region. This was primarily an agricultural
phenomenon." [B20], p. 320. He goes on to say that: "These mechanisms
(referring to a 'transport-migration cycle') were an important part of
both the ante-bellum and the later nineteenth-century economy." ibid.,
p. 236. Other evidence seems to support the contention that migration
into the regions of the U.S. where Norwegians typically went, Minnesota
and the Dakotas in the 1870's and 80's, and the Pacific region during
the first decade of the 20th century, coincided with rapid railroad development. See Frickey [B22], Chapter V, pp. 68-93.

saving in time and money over the prevalent voyage by sail-ship before

the U.S. Civil War. But the steamship ticket did not become very much

cheaper during the period up to World War I. To the extent that trav-

eling costs remained approximately the same throughout the period, it

may be regarded as a constant which will not affect the short run cost

of moving. At any rate, this factor will not be included in the empir-

ical tests because of lack of detailed information.[11]

One category of emigrants traveled on tickets sent to them from

relatives and friends already in the U.S. On the average, one-fourth to

one-third of Norwegian emigrants traveled on prepaid tickets, and Sem-

mingsen supplies some evidence of shorter run variations in the ratio of

emigrants that received prepaid tickets to the total number of emigrants

[B61], p. 184. If such fluctuations were prevalent in the case of Nor-

wegian emigration, and we don't know because of lack of comprehensive

data, it should be a function of the level of prosperity in the U.S. and

the stock of Norwegians employed there. However, since there is no in-

formation on the year to year remittance flow from the U.S. to Norway,

nor any knowledge of the exact relationship between previous migration

---

[11]Semmingsen found that a steamship ticket cost roughly 30 dollars at the beginning of the period and approximately 25 dollars during
the years 1901-03. See [B61], p. 140 and p. 399. Shorter run fluctuations, however, cannot be ruled out entirely. When, for instance, emigration in 1904 was reduced somewhat from a peak in 1903, a price-war
between the steamship companies broke out and "one could travel from
Oslo to New York for 15 dollars." ibid., p. 399 (my translation). If
this was a prevalent phenomenon, this element of the short run cost of
moving would vary inversely with the intensity of migration (and presumably unemployment) and reduce the overall short run variation in the cost
of emigration. Unfortunately, very little additional information is
available to pursue this line of thought.

and fluctuations in the flow of remittances, no empirical proxy for this factor is introduced. Presumably it will partly be taken care of by the index of the condition of prosperity in the U.S.[12]

3.1.7. SFMt, the Stock of Previous Migrants.

The role that prior Norwegian emigrants may have played for the flow of remittances has already been alluded to above. When it comes to aspects like information, the importance of living near relatives and friends, etc., it may be argued that previous emigration will directly influence the volume of labor emigration in year t up to a certain point For example, if information about the New World is exceedingly scarce, general uncertainty about conditions overseas may be so widespread so as to act as a constraint on emigration. However, once a sufficiently large stock of prior emigrants has been built up in the country of arrival, the information flowing back to the region of departure may have reached a magnitude so that additional information beyond this level will have no direct influence on emigration in year t.

By 1870, approximately the beginning of our sample period, more than 114,000 Norwegian born persons lived in the U.S. It will be assumed

---

[12]North found that remittances from the U.S. to the United Kingdom moved directly with the volume of immigration from the U.K. three years earlier. He argues that: "The most plausible explanation for this close relationship is that it took the Irish immigrants approximately three years to save passage fares for friends and family in Ireland." [B54], p. 81. However, the evidence refers to the period 1844-1860 when the means of transportation were still such that the travel to the U.S. was a major undertaking. And since the early Irish emigrants presumably were exceptionally poor, the cost of travel may have been much more of a constraint on overseas emigration than it was for other groups of emigrants later on.

in the empirical tests reported in the following section that by this
time, such a threshold level had been reached so that this factor can
be treated as a constant.

3.2. The Regression Results

According to the empirical specification of the variables set
forth in the preceding section, PYt and COt are predetermined as of
time t. Furthermore, EUSt and UNt are assumed to be exogenously determined. Finally, it is assumed that the error terms, the Vi, have constant variance and that the Vi values are pairwise uncorrelated. Under
these assumptions, ordinary least squares estimates will have the usual
desirable properties. The sample period will be 1873-1913. 1873 was
the first year for which data on PYt could be obtained. The end point
is chosen so as to exclude the abnormal war years and the succeeding
years (the 1920's) during which restrictive legislation hindered the
free flow of labor across the Atlantic.

So far I have not specified the exact functional form of the
model. With a view to determining the algebraic form of the emigration
function, there do not seem to be a priori theoretical reasons that
strongly suggest one specific form. Several alternative constructions
were tested, and the double-log form was accepted as the maintained hypothesis for the following reasons. Compared with a linear specification, the log-log form gave the best fit (as judged from the standard
errors of prediction converted to comparable measure). More importantly,
when I tested the validity of the a priori assumption of serial independence in the disturbance terms, applying the Durbin-Watson test, the

hypothesis that successive (estimated) error terms were positively auto-correlated could <u>not</u> be rejected unequivocally at a 1 percent level of significance in the case of the linear specification. This finding suggested that the autocorrelation might be due to an incorrect specification of the <u>form</u> of the relationship between the variables.[13] This suspicion was verified by the finding that in the double-log specification, the estimated Durbin-Watson statistic (computed on the basis of the anti-logs of the estimated errors so that it is comparable to the linear analogue) is such that a hypothesis of no serial correlation can be accepted at the 99 percent level of probability. See Table V-1. The regression results in this table thus refer to the following emigration function:

$$(3.2.1) \quad Ln\ Mt = Ln\ b_0 + b_1\ Ln\ PYt + b_2\ Ln\ COt + b_3\ Ln\ EUSt + b_4\ UNt + Ln\ V^{[14]}$$

The results of the regression computations reported in panel A of Table V-1 lead one to accept the basic economic model of overseas emigration set forth above. According to the F-statistic we can reject the null-hypothesis of no relationship between the endogenous variable and the whole set of explanatory variables at the 1% level of probability. Furthermore, the model predicts Norwegian emigration to the U.S. between

---

[13]This is of course a special case of the general problem of omitted variables. See for example Johnston [B34], p. 177 ff.

[14]This implies, of course, the following form

$$(3.2.1)' \quad Mt = b_0 \cdot PY_t^{b1} \cdot CO_t^{b2} \cdot EUS_t^{b3} \cdot UN_t^{b4} \cdot e^V$$

Thus it is postulated that, for instance, the long run and short run factors are multiplicative in their arguments.

TABLE V--1

REGRESSION RESULTS OF EMIGRATION MODEL 3.2.1

Dependent Variable: Mt.   Sample Period 1873-1913, N=41
Estimation Method: OLS

Panel A: EMIGRATION MODEL 3.2.1

(1) Independent Variables	(2) Regression Coefficients	(3) t-Ratios (36)	(4) Partial R^2	(5) Partial r
Constant Term	82.07			
Ln PYt	1.218	7.8139**	0.5879	0.7667
Ln COt	9.815	6.5392**	0.4921	0.7015
Ln EUSt	3.844	6.8729**	0.5213	0.7220
Ln UNt	0.4517	6.9958**	0.5291	0.7274

$\bar{R}^2 = 0.8734$; $F = 70.0016**$; D.W = 2.1223**
$(4,36)$

Panel B: ZERO ORDER CORRELATION COEFFICIENT MATRIX OF THE INDEPENDENT VARIABLES IN MODEL 3.2.1

	Ln PYt	Ln COt	Ln EUSt
Ln COt	-0.454		
Ln EUSt	0.154	-0.099	
Ln UNt	0.283	-0.111	0.400

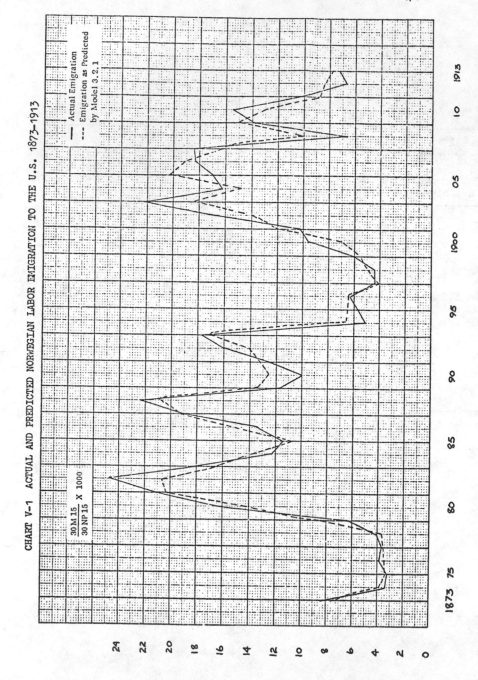

CHART V-1 ACTUAL AND PREDICTED NORWEGIAN LABOR EMIGRATION TO THE U.S. 1873-1913

30 M 15   X 1000
30 NP 15

——— Actual Emigration
----- Emigration as Predicted
      by Model 3.2.1

1873 and 1913 rather well. As judged from the coefficient of multiple determination adjusted for degrees of freedom, it accounts for more than 87 percent of the total variance in emigration of Norwegians in the prime working ages. And, as can be seen from Chart V-1 where actual and predicted year to year emigration is compared, the model can account for both the shorter cycle, the long swings and the trend in overseas emigration.

The estimated regression coefficients all have the signs that one would expect a priori, and they are all different from zero at the 99% level of significance. And since we can reject the hypothesis of serial correlation in the disturbances, the regression estimates are efficient ones. This means that the usual least-squares formulas for the sampling variances of the regression coefficients are valid, and so are the precise forms of the t and F-tests. Thus we can have full confidence in the inferences made both on the complete model and the partial regression coefficients.

Several implications of the results regarding the individual explanatory variables will now be taken up. First of all, it is seen that the average elasticity of the rate of emigration with respect to the proxy of permanent income gain has the right sign and is significantly different from zero with a probability of 99.99 percent.[15] Thus Norwe-

---

[15]The above estimates of the partial regression coefficients are, of course, equivalent to the average partial elasticities for the sample period. For example:

$$\hat{b}_1 = \frac{\partial(\text{Ln } M)}{\partial(\text{Ln } PY)} = \frac{\partial PY}{\partial M} \cdot \frac{M}{PY}$$

gians in the prime working ages responded to the increments in income
that prevailed on the other side of the Atlantic. According to these
calculations, when the past average of difference in income changed by
1 percent, the rate of Norwegian labor emigration changed by more than
1.2 percent on the average during the period in question. This finding,
then, supports the basic economic assertion that the permanent income
difference was an important explanatory factor in the case of Norwegian
historical emigration. In earlier studies, either of aggregate historical immigration to the U.S., or of the experience of individual countries, this factor has been largely assumed away or ignored. I will
briefly return to this point when alternative models are reviewed and
tested below.

A second specific finding to be noted is the statistically significant relationship between the emigration rate and the pool of Norwegian
labor in the very mobile age group. When the relative number of people
in the age-group 20 to 29 years of age grew by 1 percent, the rate of
emigration increased by almost 10 percent. Since this is the typical
time span of the "Kuznets-Sundt cycle" or long swing in demographic time
series, it may be implied that prior long swings in demographic phenomena
were indeed systematically related to emigration. This result is in contrast to an earlier empirical test of such a hypothesis by Professor
Easterlin. See [A13], especially pp. 341-48. Whereas Easterlin focused on natural increase twenty years prior to the particular year of immigration,
I argue that this empirical proxy is incorrectly specified for the test
in question. Natural increase is the balance of births and deaths in any

single year. But since the age-distribution of deaths in any particular year is heavily skewed towards the older (and non-migratory) ages, many of the deaths in year t-20 are entirely irrelevant to migration in year t. Furthermore, some of the people born in year t-20 either die off or emigrate before they reach the age of 20. A far better measure of the lagged influence of demographic changes in this instance is simply the pool of people in the age-group 20-29.[16]

Such a pool may vary in size either because of previous birth cycles, because of changes in survival rates, or because of fluctuations in prior emigration, as was discussed in Chapter II. There it was documented that all these events occurred during the period in question. Thus it is not surprising that the Norwegian emigration rate was found to be highly sensitive, ceteris paribus, to such prior demographic changes. The "demographic or cohort hypothesis" set forth briefly in a previous section, measured as an age-structure or pool component rather than as natural increase, is therefore accepted.

Thirdly, it is seen that the estimated regression coefficients of both EUS and UN have the correct signs and are significantly different from zero at the 1 percent level of significance. The proposition that employment conditions in the country of arrival are important, the most agreed upon finding in previous studies, is verified by the present model. However, another immediate implication of this finding is that "push"

---

[16]The results above are not sensitive to small changes in the age-groups included. None of the basic conclusions would be altered if the pool referred to the age groups 15 to 25, 20 to 25 or 15 to 29 years of age. All these fall within the span of the long swing which typically varied between 15 and 30 years of duration in demographic time series.

factors can be said to have contributed significantly to the determination of emigration from Norway. Confining the discussion of "pull"
versus "push" effects to the relative impact of unemployment variations
in the two regions upon the exact timing of departure, this finding
supports the general contention set forth above about the importance of
economic development in the country of departure. The period of mass
emigration to the U.S. coincided with a period of industrialization and
rapid structural change in the Norwegian economy. Thus for the predominantly rural population, migration to a Norwegian city and to the
U.S. must to some extent have been alternatives, at least in the short
run. Given the excess demand for labor in the U.S., the short run opportunity cost of emigration will vary inversely with the rate of (urban)
unemployment in Norway. As I shall argue below, previous "pull-only"
theories have implicitly assumed that the short-run opportunity cost of
emigration is always zero or insignificantly small. The above results
show that this hypothesis should be rejected as inappropriate to Norwegian historical emigration experience.

But is it not possible, one may ask, that the measured interdependence between Norwegian emigration and unemployment is merely incidental
to the fact that both are correlated with employment variations in the
U.S. so that the measured "push" effect in this sense is a spurious one?
Given that the t-ratios of both EUS and UN are both very high, or close
to 7 in absolute value, this seems to be very unlikely. However, I will
attempt to pursue this problem in more detail. I therefore proceeded to
compute third order partial correlation coefficients between the dependent

variable and the explanatory variables in addition to the zero order
correlation coefficient matrix between all the variables. See Table
V-1, panel A, column (5) and Table V-1, panel B above. The partial correlation coefficients allow us to examine the correlation between emigration and one independent variable when the other explanatory variables
are held constant, i.e., conditionally upon those other explanatory
variables taking certain fixed values.[17]

If we find that holding employment conditions in the U.S. (along
with the income difference effect and the cohort effect) fixed reduces
the correlation between unemployment in Norway and emigration, we infer
that their interdependence arises in part through the agency of employment conditions in the U.S.; and, if the partial correlation is zero or
very small, we infer that their interdependence is entirely attributable
to that agency. However, in the case of the "push" effect, it is immediately seen that this is not so at all. The third order partial correlation coefficient between Norwegian emigration and unemployment equals
0.7274. In other words, when we remove the influence of EUS (and FY and
CO) from both M and UN, very strong correlation exists between the "unexplained" residuals that remain. This confirms, then, that the effect
of Norwegian unemployment on emigration was a strong one, ceteris paribus,
and the hypothesis that the measured "push" effect is spurious or due to
intercorrelation between employment conditions in Norway and the U.S. can
be rejected unequivocally. In fact, it is seen that the third order par-

---

[17]For more details and the exact computational procedure to be
followed, see Kendall and Stuart [B35], chp. 27, esp. pp. 317-21.

tial correlation coefficient between emigration and unemployment in Norway is approximately equal in size to the third order partial correlation coefficient between emigration and employment conditions in the U.S. Thus measured, one may conclude that the "push" effect on Norwegian emigration to the U.S. was just as strong as the "pull" effect.[18]

The above discussion leads to a consideration of the more general problem of multicollinearity. From the zero order correlation coefficient matrix in panel B of Table V-1 we see that the simple correlation between the independent variables in most cases are quite low. The highest coefficient is the one between PY and CO. However, the partial correlation between emigration and these two variables is considerably higher in value, equalling 0.7667 and 0.7013 respectively. See column (5), panel A. Thus in both cases there are very strong direct association between the dependent and the independent variables. Given in addition that the two partial regression coefficients had the signs that were postulated a priori and that the estimated standard errors certainly did not "blow up", it is fair to conclude that the multicollinearity problem is not at all serious in this case.

The question now arises whether the emigration relationship, represented by equation (3.2.1), holds for two different subperiods of the entire sample period, or, alternatively, whether the basic relationship

---

[18]It is important to remember that the measure of EUS refers to employment (or output relative to trend) but that of UN equals unemployment. The size of the respective partial regression coefficients is therefore not strictly comparable. For a further discussion on this point, see Appendix B.

underwent a structural change during this time. That is to say, if we divide the entire period 1873-1913 up into two subperiods consisting of the two long swings 1873-1897 and 1898-1913 respectively, I ask whether the observations spanning the second long swing come from the same structure as the first one. Statistically this question can be answered by testing whether the two sets of observations can be regarded as belonging to the same regression model. Thus in the following I proceed to employ a "Chow-test".[19]

The method involved can be described very simply. Suppose that the observations of the long swing from 1873 to 1897 are used to estimate a regression with k parameters (k-1 coefficients plus one intercept). We are now interested in deciding whether the observations of the second long swing from 1898 to 1913 are generated from the same regression model as the first. To perform the analysis of covariance, we need the following sums of squared residuals:

SSEN, sum of squares of N = LS1 + LS2 deviations of the dependent variable from the regression estimated by LS1 + LS2 (Long Swing 1 + Long Swing 2) observations, with LS1 + LS2-k degrees of freedom.

SSELS1, sum of squares of LS1 deviations of the dependent variable from the regression estimated by the LS1 observations, i.e., the number of observations of the first long swing, with LS1-k degrees of freedom.

SSELS2, sum of squares of LS2 deviations of the dependent variable from the regression estimated by the observations of the second

---

[19] See G. C. Chow [A9], esp. pp. 602-604.

long swing, with LS2-k degrees of freedom. The ratio

$$\hat{F}_{(k,N-2k)} = \frac{(SSEN - [SSELS1 + SSELS2]) / k}{(SSELS1 + SSELS2) / N-2k}$$

follows the F distribution with k and N-2k degrees of freedom, respectively. I therefore ran the basic emigration regression on the two long swing subperiods 1873-1897 and 1898-1913, and from the results computed the sums of squared residuals from each. I found that SSELS1 = 0.995205, SSELS2 = 0.53832, and from the results of the regression exhibited in Table V-1, SSEN = 1.72884. Knowing that N = 41 and k = 5, these values are plugged into the above formula. It is found that $\hat{F}_{(5,31)}$ = 0.789653. In order to interpret the observations of the second long swing as coming from a _different_ structure than the first long swing at the 5 percent level of significance, F would have to be at least 2.53. Thus we _cannot_ reject the null hypothesis of an unchanging structure, and I therefore accept the hypothesis that Norwegian emigration to the U.S. in the years 1898-1913 was governed by the same relationship as before.

Having thus found that our maintained emigration hypothesis is not subject to structural change between tue U.S. Civil War and World War I, I now proceed to disaggregate the dependent variable as to age and sex. In doing so I attempt to ask two related questions. First, I am interested in whether the basic emigration model is valid for various subgroups of emigrants within the prime working ages. Secondly, I would like to know whether there is any difference in the response of one particular subgroup of Norwegian emigrant labor with respect to a particular predetermined variable as compared to another group. One would, for example, expect _a priori_ that young emigrants respond more strongly to a given average

permanent income difference than older workers because they have a
longer working life ahead of them.

Thus in model 3.2.3 I apply the maintained emigration hypothesis
to Norwegian emigrants to the U.S. in the age-group 15 to 29, or the
"young emigrants". The results are set forth in Table V-2, panel A.
In model 3.2.2 the dependent variable is emigrants 30 to 44 years of
age, the "middle-aged" group. See panel B of Table V-2.

It is immediately seen that the basic emigration relationship is
valid as the maintained hypothesis for both categories of labor emigrants. The economic model predicts emigration of both age-groups of
Norwegian labor well, accounting for approximately 88 and 84 percent of
total variance respectively. Furthermore, all the regression coefficients
are significantly different from zero at 1 percent level of probability.
And since the Durbin-Watson test suggests that there is no autocorrelation in the estimated residuals, one may conclude that the specification
of the aggregate model applies to both "young" and "middle-aged" emigrants.

Among the specific findings that conform with a priori expectations,
the relationship between alternative regression coefficients obtained for
the age groups 15-29 and 30-44 are of interest. Both groups are responsive to earnings differences, but the elasticity of the "young" group
with respect to this variable is significantly larger than that of the
"middle-aged" group of emigrants. This, of course, lends some additional
support to the underlying "investment-decision" approach to the study of
historical migration.

TABLE V-2

REGRESSION RESULTS OF EMIGRATION MODELS 3.2.2 AND 3.2.3.
EMIGRANTS IN PRIME WORKING AGES DISAGGREGATED AS TO AGE

Sample Period: 1873-1913.   Estimation Method: OLS

Panel A: EMIGRATION MODEL 3.2.2.   AGE GROUP 15-29

(1) Independent Variables	(2) Regression Coefficients	(3) t-Ratios (36)	(4) Partial $\bar{r}^2$	(5) Partial r
Constant Term	-81.09			
Ln PYt	1.402	8.9895**	0.6576	0.811
Ln COt	9.523	6.3401**	0.4750	0.682
Ln EUSt	3.819	6.8467**	0.5174	0.719
Ln UNt	0.4184	6.4750**	0.4867	0.698

$\bar{R}^2 = 0.8774$; $F = 72.5735^{**}$;   D.W = 2.1230**
$\quad\quad\quad\quad\quad (4,36)$

Panel B: EMIGRATION MODEL 3.2.3.   AGE GROUP 30-44

(1) Independent Variables	(2) Regression Coefficients	(3) t-Ratios	(4) Partial $\bar{r}^2$	(5) Partial r
Constant Term	-84.02			
Ln PYt	0.4823	2.7389**	0.0805	0.285
Ln COt	10.80	6.3658**	0.4773	0.691
Ln EUSt	3.834	6.0861**	0.4525	0.673
Ln UNt	0.5940	8.1405**	0.6089	0.780

$\bar{R}^2 = 0.8416$; $F = 54.1475^{**}$;   D.W = 2.0148**
$\quad\quad\quad\quad\quad (4,36)$

Notice also that both groups of emigrants are responsive to the "push" effects of Norwegian unemployment. However, the emigrants over 30 years of age are relatively more responsive to the average unemployment rate at home than the emigrants between 15 and 29, as judged from the estimated employment elasticities. One would expect that a Norwegian worker who considers himself permanently unemployed would be relatively insensitive to variations in unemployment in Norway in timing his departure. Since it is likely that a larger percentage of the younger workers below 30 experienced permanent or disguised unemployment in Norway than the older workers, the above finding conforms with what one would expect. Comparing the relative importance of employment variations in Norway and the U.s as judged from the computed third order partial correlation coefficients, in column (5) of Table V-2, it is seen that Norwegian emigration between 30 and 44 is more highly correlated with unemployment at home, ceteris paribus, than the proxy of employment variations in the U.S. The reverse is true of emigrants between 15 and 29 years of age.

As a final test of the empirical validity of our basic emigration model, I distinguish between male and female overseas migrants in prime working ages. The results of running separate regressions on emigrants disaggregated as to sex are set forth as models (3.2.4) and (3.2.5) in Table V-3. It is immediately seen that our economic emigration hypothesis can be accepted for female as well as male overseas emigrants between 15 and 44 years of age. As a matter of fact, the model can account for a slightly higher percentage of the total variance in female than in male

TABLE V-3

REGRESSION RESULTS OF EMIGRATION MODELS 3.2.4 AND 3.2.5.
EMIGRANTS IN PRIME WORKING AGES DISAGGREGATED AS TO SEX

Sample Period: 1873-1913. Estimation Method: OLS

Panel A: EMIGRATION MODEL 3.2.4. MALE EMIGRANTS 15-44

(1) Independent Variables	(2) Regression Coefficients	(3) t-Ratios (36)	(4) Partial $\bar{r}^2$	(5) Partial r
Constant Term	-82.25			
Ln PYt	1.354	7.7118**	0.5810	0.762
Ln COt	9.593	6.4568**	0.4851	0.697
Ln EUSt	4.176	6.4489**	0.4845	0.696
Ln UNt	0.4815	6.4347**	0.4832	0.695

$\bar{R}^2 = 0.8533$; $F = 59.1447^{**}$; D.W = 2.2186**
$\qquad\qquad\quad (4,36)$

Panel B: EMIGRATION MODEL 3.2.5. FEMALE EMIGRANTS 15-44

(1) Independent Variables	(2) Regression Coefficients	(3) t-Ratios (36)	(4) Partial $\bar{r}^2$	(5) Partial r
Constant Term	-68.50			
Ln PYt	0.9315	6.4057**	0.4807	0.693
Ln COt	8.162	5.4321**	0.3894	0.624
Ln EUSt	3.471	6.8304**	0.5161	0.718
Ln UNt	0.4428	7.4680**	0.5641	0.751

$\bar{R}^2 = 0.8731$; $F = 69.8080^{**}$; D.W = 1.6463**
$\qquad\qquad\quad (4,36)$

emigration, and all the separate regression coefficients can be accepted as highly statistically significant in both cases. However, as one would expect, the male elasticities are somewhat higher. So even though female emigrants responded to the specified economic and demographic factors, male emigrants were relatively more responsive to these signals. This conclusion should be modified to the extent that the female migrants between 15 and 44 years of age were dependents in the sense that they just accompanied their migrating husbands or family, or just joined the head of the houshold that had migrated earlier. For this category of female emigrants the meaning of an economic hypothesis in the sense that they are independently responding to economic signals is, perhaps, unwarranted. Unfortunately, it is not possible to separate the dependent from the independent female category in prime working ages.[20]

More generally, is it possible to isolate any one single factor that can account for the long swings (or the trend or the short cycle) in Norwegian emigration between the U.S. Civil War and World War I? In an earlier study, Professor Easterlin asked a similar question with regard to aggregate immigration to the U.S. during the same time period. See

----

[20]After 1888 there exists data on female emigrants crossclassified as to age and civil condition. For the sample period 1888 to 1913 our basic model turns out to be a good predictor of the emigration of both single and married female emigrants between 15 and 44. This may mean that the single migrants did respond to economic signals roughly in the manner suggested above, while the dependents, i.e., the married females, simply traveled with their husbands or timed their departure along the same lines as the independent emigrants. Data on Norwegian labor force participation rates of all women by age during this period is consistent with such an explanation. Between 15 and 24 (the largely unmarried group) it was almost 60 percent. For the age group 35 to 44 it was below 25 percent.

[A13], esp. pp. 341-48. In pursuing such a hypothesis I use the regression estimates to compute predicted emigration from Norway to the U.S. due to one of the explanatory variables holding the rest constant at their means. This allows us to examine and compare the separate influence of each explanatory variable on the time pattern of emigration. The results are set forth in Charts V-2 and V-3.

In Chart V-2 the fluctuations in predicted emigration due to the yearly fluctuations in employment conditions are shown. For example, series UN refers to what emigration from Norway would have been if only unemployment in Norway had varied, conditional upon the constancy of the remaining set of explanatory variables. Similarly for series EUS which refers to predicted emigration due to employment variations in the U.S., ceteris paribus. These computations show that both UN and EUS by themselves predict long swings as well as shorter cycles in Norwegian emigration. That is to say, unemployment variations in Norway during this time period would have, everything else equal, caused long swings in emigration. The same holds for the U.S. Furthermore, it is seen that there is a tendency for these two variables to reinforce each other over the long swing; i.e., a long swing in unemployment in Norway is accompanied by a long swing in employment in the U.S., so that one may argue that an inverse relationship existed between the excess demand for labor over the long swing in the two countries during this time period. Since both UN and EUS are highly statistically significant independent variables, it may be concluded that employment variations in both regions contributed to the long swing in emigration with a slightly different timing.

CHART V-2   SIMULATED NORWEGIAN LABOR EMIGRATION TO THE U.S.A.   SHORT-RUN VARIABLES VARY

(1): Norwegian unemployment (UNt) varies, while PYt, COt and EUSt are held constant at their means

(2): U. S. employment (EUSt) varies, while PYt, COt and UNt are held constant at their means

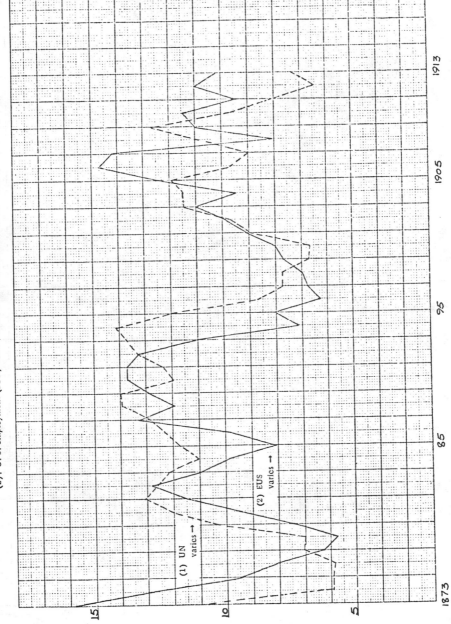

CHART V-3   SIMULATED NORWEGIAN LABOR EMIGRATION TO THE U.S.A.   LONG-RUN VARIABLES VARY

(3) : Permanent Income Differences (PYt) varies, while COt, EUSt and UNt are held constant at their means

(4) : Cohort Variable (COt) varies, while PYt, EUSt and UNt are held constant at their means

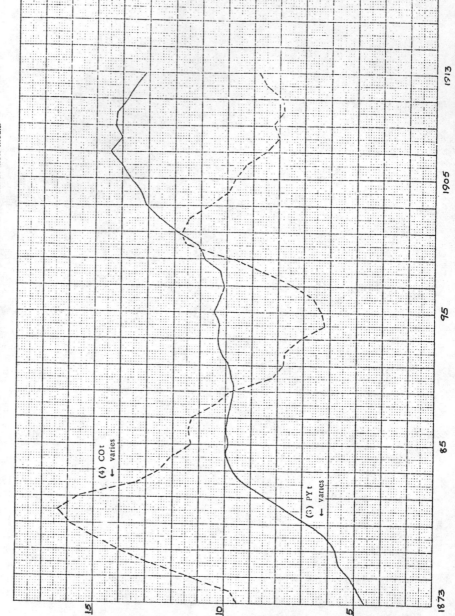

Over the short cycle, these two variables moved in considerably less harmony with each other. Consider for example the years between 1887 and 1895. In this period year to year fluctuations in UN move inversely with EUS, i.e., yearly fluctuations in excess demand for labor in both countries move synchronously. Over the short cycle, then, there is a tendency for the "push" and "pull" effects to move in opposite directions regarding Norwegian emigration to the U.S.

Consider, finally, the effects of PY and CO as depicted in Chart V-3. Again, both the permanent income variable and the cohort effect predict long swings in emigration, but with considerable timing differences. Starting from a long swing trough, the movement in both these two explanatory variables cause emigration to increase. However, the sustained increase in emigration causes, possibly in combination with other prior demographic events, the pool of potential emigrants to reach a peak while income differences between the two countries are still increasing. After this point the influence of these two factors pulls in opposite directions until the pool starts to build up again. As far as the trend in emigration is concerned, demographic factors differed from income conditions also. It is seen that the cohort effect alone would have caused a considerably higher level of emigration in the late 1870's and 1880's than during the period around the turn of the 19th century. On the other hand, income differences between the two countries became greater during the first decade of the 20th century than what they were earlier.

One may conclude then that no single variable by itself has accounted for the long swings (or the trend or the short cycle for that matter) in Norwegian emigration to the U.S. Rather it was found that all of the predetermined variables predict long swings in aggregate emigration--but with different timing. Thus the actual observed long swing pattern is due to all of the variables acting simultaneously on the endogenous variable, sometimes reinforcing each other and sometimes pulling in opposite directions. Professor Easterlin has written in regard to aggregate overseas emigration to the U.S. before World War I: "So far as this brief analysis goes, then, it leads to a view with regard to Kuznets cycles consistent with Jerome's conclusions regarding the shorter term cyclical fluctuations in immigration to the United States--that on the whole the movements were dominated by conditions in this country (the U.S.)." [A13], p. 348. While the Easterlin-Jerome view may be applicable as far as total European emigration is concerned, it is not true of emigration from Norway during this period.

V-4. Earlier Studies of Historical Overseas Migration

No comprehensive review of earlier work on historical overseas migration will be attempted in this section. Rather the focus will be on a few well-known studies in this area, the specific behavioral hypotheses set forth in these papers, and the test methods that were employed therein. Finally, I proceed to test how well these models predict Norwegian historical emigration to the U.S.[21]

---

[21]For a survey and a fairly complete bibliography of earlier studies of international migration, see B. Thomas [B68].

4.1. Business Cycle Studies

The questions raised in these types of studies, as exemplified by the classic in this field by H. Jerome, was typically: "To what extent are fluctuations in migration attributable to fluctuations in employment?" [B32], p. 239, and "...are fluctuations in the tide of migration due primarily to conditions at home or in the country of destination?" ibid., p. 153 . Fluctuations typically means business cycle fluctuations, thus these early studies had as their main objective to explain the short fluctuations in migration. Without specifying the a priori theoretical-behavioral considerations that supposedly underlie such relationships, these investigators proceeded to look at the data. Consequently, the time series were smoothed, typically by seven year moving averages which were taken to be the trend of the series, and the analysis proceeded in units of standard deviation from such trends. The dependent variable was the total number of migrants or the total number of male migrants, and no attempts were made to separate labor in prime working ages from dependent emigrants. The economic series used, as proxies for employment variations, were typically annual series of pig iron production or annual comparable business cycle indexes.[22]

The analytical methods used in these studies were graphical or simple correlation analysis. The time series were plotted on a graph and compared, or zero order correlation coefficients were computed. Some of the results, especially those obtained by Jerome, are well known. Positive

---

[22]A good summary table of the various series used and the main results can be found in D. S. Thomas [B69], p. 91 and pp. 167-68.

correlation was found between the U.S. series and immigration while the
simple correlation coefficient between emigration from a particular
country and a business cycle index there was generally lower and in two
instances had a positive sign. On this basis a "pull-only" interpretation was generally accepted.[23] The only previous economic analysis of
Norwegian emigration to the U.S. by Skaug [B62] employs graphical analysis only, and the conclusions reached are very similar to those of
Jerome.[24]

No one doubts that conditions in the U.S. were of importance, and
on this point there is little disagreement as such. However, if the hypothesis is "pull-only", I object to the use of simple (or zero-order)
correlation techniques on methodological grounds. It is well known, as
was discussed in some detail above, that such statistical measures do not
separate out the effects of individual factors. This makes it impossible
to use statistical tests of significance unless the "pull" and "push"
factors which may influence the variations in emigration vary entirely

---

[23]Jerome computes correlation coefficients only for emigration
from three countries, namely the United Kingdom, Germany and Italy, and
in the case of British emigration the evidence is not conclusive. See
[B32], p. 182. D. S. Thomas, in her study of Swedish emigration to the
U.S., found significant negative correlation between Swedish business
cycles and emigration as well as positive correlation with U.S. indices
[B69], p. 167.

[24]The emigration series used was total emigration per 1000 of population, and the business cycle indexes were respectively: the Ogburn-
Thomas index, U.S. imports, Norwegian foreign trade per inhabitant, and
Norwegian money circulation per inhabitant. These were graphed as deviations from seven year moving averages and compared. From this, Skaug concludes that: "On the whole it must be said that it is the fluctuations
of the business cycles in America that have caused the greatest fluctuations in the emigration from Norway." [B62], p. 68.

independently of each other--a very unlikely situation. The direct relationship between a change in emigration and business conditions in the
home country may be blurred by an offsetting influence of conditions in
the U.S. In other words, a positive or lack of observed negative relationship between a business cycle index in the country of departure and
emigration, as measured by a zero order correlation coefficient, is entirely consistent with a true direct negative relationship as measured
by the partial correlation coefficient which would reveal a "push" effect
independently of the "pull" effect. Thus I contend that Jerome's conclusion that: "...the immigration movement into the United States is on the
whole dominated by conditions in the United States" ibid., p. 208, is too
strong in view of the empirical test methods he used. D. S. Thomas, on
the other hand, seems to be more aware of the limitations of simple correlation analysis, and her conclusions differ accordingly from those of
Jerome.[25]

In view of these early studies of historical migration to the U.S.,
it may be of interest to see how well variations in employment conditions

---

[25]Thomas states that: "From a methodological point of view it is
dangerous to give so definite interpretation to difference between (simple) correlation coefficients. We are on far safer ground if we system-
atize the observed variations, year by year, in terms of corresponding
or non-corresponding cyclical phases in Sweden and America." [B59] p. 169.
When this is done, the much weaker conclusion emerges that: "the most
consistent increases in emigration occurred when pull and push coincided;
the most consistent decline, when there was no pull in America coincident
with no push from Sweden. Even more revealing is the fact that the pull
from America was quite ineffective in years of prosperity (no push) in
Sweden; and the push in Sweden was similarly ineffective when there was
depression (no pull) in America." op. cit., p. 169.

alone can predict Norwegian emigration during this time period. The following hypotheses will therefore be tested below:

(4.1.1) $Mt = a + b_1 EUSt + ut$

and

(4.1.2) $Mt = a + b_1 EUSt + b_2 UNt + ut$

These will be referred to as the Jerome model and the Thomas model respectively.

4.2. Distributed Lag Models of Overseas Migration .

Two such models have been suggested in recent work on historical overseas migration. As will be shown below, Kelley applied essentially a version of the adaptive expectation model to an analysis of British immigration to Australia. See [A20]. Wilkinson, on the other hand, entertains a stock-adjustment hypothesis in his study of Swedish emigration to the U.S. [A43]. These models will now be examined and their analytical content compared with my own basic migration hypothesis.

Kelley starts out by regressing annual net immigration from Britain to Australia on unemployment rates in both countries. Despite the fact that both explanatory variables are found to be statistically significant at the 95 percent level of probability, "push" factors are dropped from the subsequent analysis. See [A20], p. 342. He then goes on to consider several "pull-only" models arguing that: "..., it might be proposed that the migrant's assessment of expected Australian conditions on arrival is formulated on the basis of more than existing employment opportunities; a distributed lag response may be a better description of the decision-making procedure." ibid., p. 343. (The italics are mine.) Several suggestions as to the nature of the migrant's decision function are set forth. One such specification is simply

$$(4.2.1) \quad M_t = a + b_1 E_t + b_2 E_{t-1} + U_t \quad [26]$$

where E_t refers to employment conditions in the region of arrival.

However, the formulation that Kelley accepts as his maintained hypothesis, largely on empirical grounds, "assumes that the weight migrants attach to subsequent unemployment rates in assessing expected labor market conditions declines geometrically through time...." [A20], p. 345. The basic behavioral relationship of such a model must be that actual migration in year t depends on the expected future value of employment in the region of arrival in that year, i.e.,

$$(4.2.2) \quad M_t = a + b E^e_t + u_t$$

where E^e_t = expected future employment opportunities in the region of arrival in year t. How are expectations about future employment opportunities in the country of immigration formed? According to Kelley's verbal statement, the expectation hypothesis held is

$$(4.2.3) \quad E^e_t = c E^e_{t-1} + (1-c) E_{t-1} \quad , \quad 0 \leqq c < 1.$$

In other words, the currently held expectations about the future value of employment is a weighted average of the expectation held last period and

---

[26]This version refers to Kelley's model (3b). See [A20], p. 345.

the actual observable value of employment in year t-1.[27] In order to
compare the conceptual meaning of Kelley's distributed lag model in more
detail with our own, consider the expectation hypothesis set forth in
(4.2.3) above expressed in the following equivalent form:

$$(4.2.4) \qquad E^e t = 1-c \sum_{i=1}^{n} c^i Et-i \text{ , where } i=1,2....n \text{ .}$$

Substituting this expression for $E^e t$ into (4.2.2) we get

$$(4.2.5) \qquad Mt = a + b(1-c) \sum_{i=1}^{n} c^i Et-i + u$$

which is the underlying behavioral relationship that is postulated by
Kelley. It can now be seen that this is a "pull-only" model of overseas
migration in that it hypothesizes that expected employment opportunities
in the region of arrival is the only explanatory variable. Furthermore,
these expected opportunities are in turn determined by a (large) number
of past values of employment conditions in that region measured as the
actual rate of unemployment in the years t-i.

The general adaptive expectation hypothesis attributes these lags
in the adjustment to uncertainty and the discounting of current (or very
recent) information. When this general framework is applied to an analy-

---

[27]The expectation hypothesis implicitely assumed in Kelley's model
(3b) restated as (4.2.1) above is much simpler and equals

$$(4.2.3') \qquad E^e t = b_1 Et + b_2 Et-1 \text{ .}$$

However, as mentioned above, Kelley regards (4.2.3) to be an improvement
over (4.2.3'). See ibid., p. 345.

sis of overseas migration, a mode of formations of expectations on the part of migrants concerning future employment opportunities is assumed. But now we are very close to using expected employment opportunities interchangeably with "normal" or long run employment opportunities. In fact, such a concept seems hard to rationalize in other terms than as a migrant's notion of the "normal" employment opportunities in the region of arrival, since it is hypothesized to be a function of a (large) number of past unemployment rates, each one only representing a very short run market phenomenon. Yet such an expectation model of migration: "... proposes that the timing of migration is most sensitive to expected employment opportunities...." [A20], p. 345.

Conceptually, then, this is very different from my own migration hypothesis. My general point has been that current employment conditions are the most important short term variables affecting fluctuation in the timing of a migration stream from a pool of potential migrants whose size is basically determined by other factors. Surely long term expectations of employment opportunities, as distinct from income, could hardly be a plausible determinant of such a pool unless one states that income differences, demographic factors, etc., do not change, even in the long run, and can therefore be taken as constants. Since Kelley tests his model on yearly data unadjusted for trend and long swings for the seventy years 1865-1935, this seems indeed to be the implicit assumption underlying his theory. A priori, I contend that it is fundamentally implausible except in such a context. The question then becomes how well the model performs empirically. I will therefore proceed to show that Kelley's empirical conclusions regarding his distributed lag "pull-only" model of British immigration to Australia may be invalid for methodological reasons as well.

In order to do that, consider his basic model as set forth in equations (4.2.1) and (4.2.3) above. Now we substitute the expression for $E^e t$ given in (4.2.3) into (4.2.2) and get

(4.2.6) $Mt = a + b (cE^e t-1 + (1-c)Et-1) + ut$.

Lag equation (4.2.2) one period and rearrange it. We have

(4.2.7) $bE^e t-1 = Mt-1 - a - ut-1$.

Substituting this expression for $bE^e t-1$ into (4.2.6) gives

(4.2.8) $Mt = a(1-c) + cMt-1 + b(1-c) Et-1 + (ut - cut-1)$.

Here all the variables except the error terms are observable. Furthermore, this reduced form equation is equivalent to Kelley's distributed lag model (3c). See ibid., p. 345. I will refer to (4.2.8) as Kelley Model 2. He proceeds to estimate Kelley Model 1, presented as equation (4.2.1) above, and Model 2 by ordinary least squares. Model 1 is found to possess considerable autocorrelation in the residuals, the estimated Durbin-Watson statistic being equal to 0.84, which suggests that Model 1 is underspecified, or alternatively that a different formulation of the adjustment process, for instance the one set forth in Model 2, might be more appropriate. Since estimation of the second model results in a Durbin-Watson statistic of 1.67, this model is accepted as the maintained hypothesis largely because of the "improvement" in the estimated Durbin-Watson statistic. When, however, as in the case of Model 2, lagged endogenous variables are included in an equation estimated by ordinary least squares, the Durbin-Watson statistic is asymptotically biased towards 2, the value which it should have if no serial correlation in the error terms is in fact present.[28] In the case of Model 2, then, one cannot guard against serial correlation by observing the Durbin-Watson statistic. Thus the criteria Kelley uses for accepting it as the true model is inappropriate.

To see in more detail what is involved, consider the expression of the error term in equation (4.2.8). Notice that if it is believed that the disturbances u_t and u_s are independent for $t \neq s$, as is a standard assumption in regression models, the disturbances in the empirically estimatable equation (4.2.8) do not have this property as long as c is different from zero. For the disturbances in (4.2.8) include $u_t - cu_{t-1}$, which must be serially dependent on $u_{t-1} - cu_{t-2}$ because both contain u_{t-1}. Hence M_{t-1} cannot be predetermined in (4.2.8). Furthermore, it is well known that serial correlation in the disturbances in distributed lag models is likely to lead to inconsistent estimates. Moreover, in the likely case of positive serial correlation, the estimate of the coefficient of M_{t-1} obtained from ordinary least squares will be biased upwards, even asymptotically. The same source of the upward bias in the coefficient of the lagged dependent variable will lead to a downward bias in the serial

---

[28] For further discussion of the use of the Durbin-Watson statistic in inappropriate situations, see for example Nerlove and Wallis [A31].

correlation of the estimated residuals. Thus the upward bias of the Durbin-Watson statistic.[29]

On the other hand, suppose, as would seem most unlikely, that the disturbance u were serially autocorrelated as in

(4.2.9)   ut = cut-1 + vt

with an autoregression coefficient precisely equal to the expectation coefficient c, where vt is a random disturbance independent as among different time periods. Only then will ut - cut-1 be serially independent. In other words, unless the first order autocorrelation coefficient of the errors in (4.2.2) happens to equal c, the errors in the reduced form (4.2.8) will be autocorrelated. Given Kelley's estimation method, then, the validity of his empirical results regarding Model 2 rests entirely on that very unlikely assumption.

In view of the preceding critical discussion of previous "pull-only" models of historical overseas migration, I proceeded to test how well such models were able to predict Norwegian overseas emigration to the U.S. The results are set forth in panels A through C of Table V-4.

It is immediately seen that the Jeromian model (4.1.1) and the Kelley 1 model (4.2.1) possess considerable serial correlation which immediately suggests that both these models are underspecified. More importantly perhaps, notice that the regression coefficient of UESt-1, i.e., employment variations in the U.S. one year prior to emigration, with respect to

---

[29]For an analytical derivation of the bias, see Griliches [A16], pp. 36-37 and the references contained therein.

TABLE V-4

REGRESSION RESULTS OF "PULL-ONLY" EMIGRATION MODELS.

Dependent Variable: Norwegian Emigrants 15-44,
Sample Period: 1873-1913, Estimation Method: OLS

Panel A: THE JEROME MODEL. EMIGRATION MODEL 4.1.1

(1) Independent Variables	(2) Regression Coefficients	(3) t-Ratios (39)	(4) Partial $\bar{r}^2$	(5) Partial r
Constant Term	-18.42			
EUSt	0.2339	4.8042**	0.3557	0.596

$\bar{R}^2 = 0.3557$; $F = 23.0805**$; D.W = 0.5745
  (1,39)

Panel B: KELLEY MODEL 1. EMIGRATION MODEL 4.2.1

(1) Independent Variables	(2) Regression Coefficients	(3) t-Ratios (38)	(4) Partial $\bar{r}^2$	(5) Partial r
Constant Term	-15.49			
EUSt	0.2951	4.3625**	0.2986	0.547
EUSt-1	- 0.0860	1.2911	0.0	0.0

$\bar{R}^2 = 0.3665$; $F = 12.5712**$; D.W = 0.7313
  (2,38)

Panel C: KELLEY MODEL 2. EMIGRATION MODEL 4.2.8

(1) Independent Variables	(2) Regression Coefficients	(3) t-Ratios (38)	(4) Partial $\bar{r}^2$	(5) Partial .r
Constant Term	7.905			
EUSt-1	-0.0689	1.2072	0.0	0.0
Mt-1	0.8418	5.5369**	0.4174	

$\bar{R}^2 = 0.4728$; $F = 18.9331**$; D.W = 1.6814
  (2,38)

Norwegian emigration in prime working ages has the wrong sign and is not significantly different from zero even at the 20 percent level of significance, both in Models (4.2.1) and (4.2.8). Furthermore, the partial correlation coefficient of EUSt-1 with respect to Mt is 0.0. See panels B and C, columns (3) and (5). This finding renders it highly unlikely that the misspecification of Kelley Model 1, as applied to Norwegian overseas emigration to the U.S., is due to the fact that: "the weight migrants attach to subsequent employment conditions in assessing expected labor market conditions declines geometrically through time." [A20], p. 345.

Consider instead the following alternative explanation. It is simply that the true equation is <u>not</u> a distributed lag model, but just a regular relation between contemporaneous variables as follows:

(4.2.10) $M_t = a + bEUS_t + u_t$

<u>with</u> serially correlated residuals

(4.2.11) $u_t = cu_{t-1} + w_t$

due to specification errors such as leaving out any serially correlated variable (e.g. trend) from the original equation. If we estimate

(4.2.12) $M_t = a + bEUS_t + cM_{t-1} + v_t$

introducing the irrelevant M_{t-1} variable into the estimating equation, we will usually get significant and sensible coefficients and will reduce the serial correlation in the estimated residuals. In such a case, an expection model "will work" even though it is incorrect. I will now proceed to show that this is indeed the case when it is applied to Norwegian emigration.

Consider the "serial correlation alternative" set forth in equations (4.2.10) and (4.2.11). Lag equation (4.2.10) one period and insert the resulting expression for u_{t-1} into (4.2.11). We get

$$(4.2.13) \quad u_t = c(M_{t-1} - a - bEUS_{t-1}) + W_t .$$

Now substitute this expression for u_t into (4.2.10). We have

$$(4.2.14) \quad M_t = a(1-c) + bEUS_t + cM_{t-1} - cbEUS_{t-1} + W_t .$$

Thus, if the coefficient of EUS_{t-1} is <u>negative</u> and <u>significant</u> when added to the expectation model and approximately equal to $-bc$, it may be concluded that an expectation specification implied by the reduced form equation (4.2.12) is in error. To test this hypothesis I proceeded to estimate equations (4.2.12) and (4.2.14), and the results are exhibited in Table V-5.

It is immediately seen from this table that we can accept model (4.2.14) or the "serial correlation alternative" rather than model (4.2.12). The estimated regression coefficient of EUS_{t-1} is approximately equal to minus the product of the coefficients of EUS_t and M_{t-1}; i.e., $-(0.2547 \times 0.8337) \approx -0.2201$. See column (2) of panel B in Table V-5. Furthermore, since there is no alternative explanation for a statistically significant negative coefficient of the lagged employment variable in the region of arrival, I reject the expectation model and accept the serial correlation one. This is entirely consistent with the previous acceptance of

TABLE V-5

REGRESSION TESTS OF AN ADAPTIVE EXPECTATION MODEL VERSUS ITS SERIAL CORRELATION ALTERNATIVE

Dependent Variable, Sample Period and Estimation
Method as in Table V-4

Panel A: AN ADAPTIVE EXPECTATION MODEL. EMIGRATION MODEL 4.2.12

(1) Independent Variables	(2) Regression Coefficients	(3) t-Ratios (38)	(4) Partial $\bar{r}^2$	(5) Partial r
Constant Term	-10.73			
EUSt	0.1365	2.7033**	0.1172	
Mt-1	0.5425	4.0791**	0.2679	

$\bar{R}^2 = 0.5402$; $F = 24.4994^{**}$; D.W = 1.1024
$(2,38)$

Panel B: THE SERIAL CORRELATION ALTERNATIVE. EMIGRATION MODEL 4.2.14

(1) Independent Variables	(2) Regression Coefficients	(3) t-Ratios (37)	(4) Partial $\bar{r}^2$	(5) Partial r
Constant Term	-1.84			
EUSt	0.2547	4.9088**	0.3453	
Mt-1	0.8337	6.0184**	0.4537	
EUSt-1	-0.2201	4.0346**	0.2492	

$\bar{R}^2 = 0.6721$; $F = 28.3256^{**}$; D.W = 1.6801
$(3,37)$

model (3.2.1) as our maintained emigration hypothesis since this model includes other (trend) variables than U.S. employment variations. In any event, one may conclude that the true model of Norwegian overseas emigration to the U.S. is _not_ a distributed lag model along the lines suggested by Kelley's work.

In recent work on Swedish emigration to the U.S., Wilkinson entertains the hypothesis that: "Employment opportunities in both the home and the country of destination are primarily responsible for the fluctuations in emigration." [A43], p. 33. His model differs from the one suggested earlier by D. S. Thomas in that: "... employment opportunities in the United States and in Sweden are thought to influence emigration not only in the given year but also in subsequent years at a declining rate." op. cit., p. 34. Exactly why this should be so is not made explicit by the author, and we, once more, are only presented with the estimates of a reduced form equation. I will therefore attempt to make more explicit the behavioral hypotheses that may lie behind the equation that Wilkinson employs.[30]

---

[30]It should be stressed that the following interpretation is mine since the only clue, as far as I can see, that Wilkinson gives as to the conceptual meaning of his model is the statement that: "This model employs a distributed lag after Koyck in that the dependent variable, emigration from Sweden to the United States, is entered with a one year lag as an independent variable." [A43], p. 34. Koyck, in his well-known book, studied the reaction of capacity to changes in output in various industries. See [B39]. This is generally known as the stock-adjustment model, and I therefore presume that Wilkinson applies a similar conceptual framework in his analysis of historical overseas migration.

Let the unobservable <u>desired</u> level of migration M_t^d depend on current employment conditions in both the region of arrival and departure as follows:

$$(4.2.15) \quad M_t^d = a + b_1 EUSt + b_2 UNt + ut .$$

Assume, furthermore, that the adjustment of the actual level of migration Mt toward the desired level M_t^d is not an instantaneous process. In particular, assume that during a given year t only a certain fraction 1-d of the difference between the desired level M_t^d and the initial level Mt-1 is made up. Thus

$$(4.2.16) \quad Mt - Mt-1 = (1 - d)(M_t^d - Mt-1) , \quad 0 \leqq d < 1 .$$

Now substituting for the expression for M_t^d given in (4.2.15) into (4.2.16) gives the following equation:

$$(4.2.17) \quad Mt = (1-d) a \quad (1-d) b_1 EUSt + (1-d) b_2 UNt + dMt-1 + (1-d) ut .$$

This reduced form equation in actual observable variables and disturbances is equivalent to the one estimated by Wilkinson.[31]

There are two key notions underlying such a model. First, what does it mean to talk about the desired level of migration M_t^d ? Making no claim of exhausting the various possibilities, the analogy that makes most sense in the distinction made between short run and long run equilibrium output

---

[31]Except that Wilkinson's version is in a double-log form, see ibid., p. 34. In the empirical tests of this model below I will therefore follow Wilkinson in this respect.

in production theory. In other words, long run equilibrium migration depends on actual employment conditions according to (4.2.15). This is a
very different hypothesis from the one I proposed; indeed, this is almost
the permanent income model turned on its head.

Secondly, it is assumed that in each period actual migration is adjusted in proportion to the difference between long run equilibrium or
desired migration and actual migration according to (4.2.16). The justification for a lag in adjustment is now presumably of a technological-
institutional nature. Once the decision to emigrate is made, some people
cannot leave immediately, the boat trip to the U.S. takes time, etc. Since
the time periods employed in the empirical work refers to the calendar
year, and since for example the boat trip across the Atlantic took two
weeks, one would think that almost complete adjustment within a year would
be quite possible.

In a recent paper on the use of Markov processes in the analysis of
migration, Kelley and Weiss point out that the stock adjustment model is,
indeed, the "economic" analogue of the Markov process. They argue that:
"An implication is that the stock adjustment mechanism is subject to many
of the same criticisms that we have developed concerning the simple Markov
process. Such simple analytic mechanisms may, of course, yield in some
circumstances good approximations to economic phenomena, but it appears that
they imply a questionable economic model at least in the analysis of migration." [A22], p. 291.

Having thus criticized the Wilkinson stock adjustment hypothesis on
analytical grounds, I now proceed to test the predictive power of the Thomas-

Wilkinson type models as applied to Norwegian overseas emigration. Notice
that the disturbance $(1-d)$ ut in equation $(4.2.17)$ is free of serial dependence if ut is. Provided, then, that ut is random and with no
serial dependence, an ordinary least squares estimator should yield unbiased estimates of the reduced form equation $(4.2.17)$. However, if this
is not the case, Mt-1 is not a predetermined variable and so a bias in
estimating d will occur using OLS. The econometric results are set forth
Table V-6.

Consider first a double-log version of the D. S. Thomas "unemployment-only" model as specified in equation $(4.1.2)$ above. From panel A in
Table V-6 it can be seen that current unemployment variations alone lead
to an underspecified model of unsmoothed yearly overseas emigration of
Norwegians in prime working ages. Consult the Durbin-Watson statistic
which is only 0.8766. We therefore proceed to test the hypothesis that
such an incomplete specification is due to the possibility of only partial
adjustment to current employment conditions as suggested by Wilkinson.
The estimates of his model are set forth in panel B of Table V-6.

Notice that the regression coefficient of the lagged dependent
variable Mt-1 is barely statistically significant at the 5 percent level
of probability, thus it is insignificant at the 1 percent level. Secondly,
the fit of equation $(4.2.17)$ is not very much improved as compared with
the D. S. Thomas model. Thirdly, it implies a relatively rapid rate of adjustment of about 70 percent per year so that the long-run coefficients
as estimated from the Wilkinson specification are very close in absolute
value to the contemporaneous response measured by the simple Thomas

TABLE V-6

REGRESSION TESTS OF THE D. S. THOMAS AND WILKINSON UNEMPLOYMENT ONLY EMIGRATION MODELS

Dependent Variable, Sample Period and Estimation
Method as in Table V-5

Panel A: A THOMAS DOUBLE-LOG MODEL. EMIGRATION MODEL 4.1.2

(1) Independent Variables	(2) Regression Coefficients	(3) t-Ratios (38)	(4) Partial $\bar{r}^2$	(5) Partial r
Constant Term	-16.00			
Ln EUSt	3.812	4.152**	0.5206	0.722
Ln UNt	0.558	5.215**	0.6170	0.786

$\bar{R}^2 = 0.6381$; $F = 37.1481**$; $D.W = 0.8766$
$\qquad\qquad\qquad (2,38)$

Panel B: THE WILKINSON STOCK-ADJUSTMENT MODEL. EMIGRATION MODEL 4.2.17

(1) Independent Variables	(2) Regression Coefficients	(3) t-Ratios (37)
Constant Term	-11.47	
Ln EUSt	2.729	2.653**
Ln UNt	0.4050	3.187**
Ln Mt-1	0.293	2.052*

$\bar{R}^2 = 0.6657$; $F = 28.2090**$; $D.W = 1.1567$
$\qquad\qquad\qquad (2,37)$

model.[32] All this may suggest that the true equation is, once more, not a distributed lag model in unemployment variables, but just a regular relation between current migration and employment conditions with serially correlated residuals due to left-out variables. In such a case, as was discussed in some detail above, the OLS estimate of the adjustment coefficient d is likely to be biased upwards. If the true estimate of d, $\hat{d} = 0$, then a model postulating only partial adjustment to current employment conditions can be rejected.

Consider, therefore, the following alternative to equation (4.2.15) above:

$$(4.2.18) \quad M_t^d = a + b_1 PYt + b_2 COt + b_3 EUSt + b_4 UNt + Wt .$$

Substituting this expression for M_t^d into equation (4.2.16) above gives us

$$(4.2.19) \quad Mt = (1-d)a + (1-d)b_1 PYt + (1-d)b_2 COt + (1-d)b_3 EUSt + (1-d)b_4 UNt$$
$$+ dMt-1 + (1-d)wt .$$

The specific hypothesis to be tested is the null hypothesis

$H_0 : d = 0$ against the alternative that

$H_1 : 0 < d < 1$

If we can accept the null-hypothesis that $d = 0$, then the adjustment hy-

---

[32]I.e., the long-run coefficients b_1 and b_2 as specified in (4.2.15) equal respectively $2.729/(1 - 0.293) \cong 3.89$ and $0.4050/(1 - 0.293)$ 0.578 as computed from the estimates of the reduced form equation (4.2.17) where $\hat{d} = 0.293$. These long-run estimates are very close to the contemporaneous coefficients of 3.812 and 0.558 as estimated from the Thomas specification (4.1.2).

TABLE V-7

REGRESSION TESTS OF THE MOE PARTIAL STOCK-ADJUSTMENT MODEL.
EMIGRATION MODEL 4.2.19

Dependent Variable, Sample Period and Estimation
Method as in Table V-6

(1) Independent Variables	(2) Regression Coefficients	(3) t-Ratios (35)	(4) Partial r^2	(5) Partial r
Constant Term	-80.10			
Ln PYt	1.183	6.7900**	0.5068	0.712
Ln COt	9.743	6.3878**	0.4723	0.687
Ln EUSt	3.673	5.4670**	0.3836	0.620
Ln UNt	0.431	5.5082**	0.3878	0.623
Ln Mt-1	0.047	0.4679	0.0	0.0

$\bar{R}^2 = 0.8706$; $F = 54.8300^{**}$; $D.W = 2.1488^{**}$
$(5,35)$

pothesis set forth in (4.2.16) simply states that $M_t^d = M_t$. Such a finding would, furthermore, lead us to believe that the misspecification of the Thomas model was due to left-out variables rather than partial adjustment to current employment conditions. The regression estimates of (4.2.19) (in log-log form) are exhibited in Table V-7.

It is immediately seen from the t-ratios in column (3) of this table that we can, indeed, accept the null-hypothesis that the coefficient of the lagged dependent variable is equal to zero. Notice, furthermore, that the lagged emigration variable exhibits no independent explanatory power and that the fourth-order partial correlation coefficient between M_t and M_{t-1} equals 0. Consult columns (4) and (5). We can therefore reject the Wilkinson partial stock-adjustment hypothesis, as applied to overseas Norwegian labor emigration, on empirical grounds. And since emigration model (4.2.19) is exactly equal to emigration model (3.2.1) except for the inclusion of M_{t-1}, the results exhibited in Table V-7 provide an independent test which confirms the validity of the acceptance of emigration model (3.2.1) as the maintained hypothesis regarding Norwegian emigration to the United States between the U.S. Civil War and World War I.

V-5. Conclusions

The major objective of this chapter has been to analyze the substantial overseas emigration of Norwegian labor during one of the most important periods of demographic redistribution in recorded history. In order to do so I developed a behavioral model of labor emigration and tested its validity.

Our basic migration hypothesis stated that the propensity to migrate was in the long run a function of expected income relatives and the supply of young potential migrants. The short run adjustment of such regional disequilibrium would be dependent on the short run cost of moving.

This model was found to predict Norwegian labor emigration to the U.S. between 1873 and 1913 very well. Specifically, all the estimated regression coefficients have the correct signs and are significantly different from zero at the 1 percent level of probability. One immediate implication of this is that "push" factors can be said to have contributed significantly to the determination of emigration from Norway. Confining the discussion of "pull" versus "push" effects to the relative impact of unemployment variations in the two regions upon the exact timing of departure, this finding is readily interpreted. The period of mass emigration to the U.S. coincided with a period of industrialization and rapid structural change in the Norwegian economy. Thus for the predominantly rural population, migration to a Norwegian city and to the U.S. must to some extent have been alternatives, at least in the short run. It was argued that this possibility has been largely overlooked in much of the earlier work on historical overseas emigration. Previous "pull-only" theories have implicitely assumed that the opportunity cost of emigration is always zero or insignificantly small. This hypothesis was tested and rejected as inappropriate to Norwegian historical emigration experience.

A second specific finding to be noted is the significant causal relationship between the rate of emigration and the relative number of people in the age-group 20-29. Since this is the typical time span of the Kuznets cycle or long swing in demographic phenomena, it may be implied that prior long swings in demographic phenomena were systematically related to emigration. This result is in contrast to an earlier empirical test of such a hypothesis by Professor Easterlin relating to aggregate immigration into the U.S. I argued that the empirical proxy that Easterlin used was incorrectly specified for the test in question. Besides, I contend that his method of comparing peaks and troughs in smoothed time series cannot rigorously establish causality or lack of such.

When the total number of Norwegian emigrants between the ages of 15 and 44 were divided into various subgroups according to their age, sex and civil condition, the same basic explanatory equation was found to give excellent statistical results in every case. Among the specific findings that conformed with a priori expectations, the relationship between alternative regression coefficients obtained for the age groups 15-29 and 30-44 was found to be of interest. Both groups were responsive to earnings differentials, but the elasticity of the "young" group with respect to this variable was significantly larger than that of the "middle-aged" group of emigrants. This of course lends some additional support to the underlying "investment-decision" approach to the study of historical migration.

More generally, I found that no single variable by itself could account for the long swings (or the trend or the short cycle for that matter) in Norwegian emigration. This conclusion rests on the use of the regression estimates to compute predicted emigration due to one of the explanatory variables holding the rest constant at their means. It was found that all of the predetermined variables predicted long swings in aggregate emigration--but with different timing. Thus the actual observed long swing pattern is due to all of the variables acting simultaneously on the endogenous variable, sometimes reinforcing each other and sometimes pulling in opposite directions.

Finally, several previous "unemployment-only" models of historical overseas emigration were reviewed and tested for their applicability regarding the Norwegian emigration stream during the same time period within which these models have generally been applied. Including only unemployment variations as explanatory variables was found to result in underspecified models of emigration from Norway. And the hypothesis that emigrants, for various reasons, respond to lagged employment conditions, as has been suggested by the work of Kelley and Wilkinson, was rejected as inappropriate in the case of Norwegian historical emigration to the U.S. Such findings lend some additional support to our contention that current employment conditions were the most important short term variables affectings fluctuations in the timing of a migration stream from a pool of potential migrants whose size is basically determined by other factors. In view of all this, a suggestion for further research in this area would be to apply our model to a larger sample of nations.

In concluding, it may be appropriate to point out some of the limitations of my own of historical overseas emigration. First, our data, although reasonably good as historical indicators go, is of course in several respects quite crude by modern standards and based on incomplete primary statistical material. Secondly, and perhaps more importantly, the analysis was carried out in terms of a partial equilibrium model. For example, it

was assumed that variations in the rate of unemployment in Norway was
exogenously determined. To the extent that unemployment variations in
year t were influenced by emigration in the same year, our statistical
results contain some Haavelmo-bias due to well-known simultaneous equation
problems. Ideally, it would of course have been preferable to construct
a model in which unemployment in Norway enters as an endogenous variable
and where our explanatory equation that relates to the functioning of a
particular market is just a subset of a larger macro-economic model. Although this was clearly beyond the scope of the present study, this is an
ambitious possibility for further research on overseas emigration, labor
markets, and on Norwegian historical economic development more generally.
The returns from such an undertaking may, however, be very high indeed.

CHAPTER VI

CONCLUSIONS AND SOME SUGGESTIONS FOR FURTHER RESEARCH

"A moment's reflection on the part of
any economist should convince him that
to the extent that economic history
moves beyond the simple cataloguing of
facts, it must meet of necessity the
same set of standards that we attempt
to impose by the use of scientific
methods in economics."

Douglass C. North.
"The State of Economic History"
American Economic Review,Vol. LV, No. 2
(May, 1965), p. 66.

"The novel element in the work of the
new economic historians is their approach to measurement and theory."

Robert W. Fogel.
"The Reunification of Economic History
with Economic Theory"
American Economic Review, Vol. LV, No. 2
(May, 1965), p. 92.

For the purposes of this very brief summary, I will concentrate on
two specific aspects of the study. The first is the analysis of the determinants of aggregate births in Norway before 1865, when internal and external migration was still of small quantitative significance. Thus the
object of this part of the study was in effect the successful prediction
of births in a closed population. A second major objective of the dissertation was the explanation of the massive emigration from Norway that took
place after 1865. The study was carried out with the help of econometric
models in which variables describing economic conditions and the age struc-

ture of the population in family formation and migratory ages were assumed to be predetermined.

The advantages of such possible "novel elements" were argued at
some length above, especially in Chapters III and V. And, as a biproduct,
some of the "conventional wisdom" of previous research in the field was
challenged in view of the econometric results of this study. Thus, it is
felt that I have provided a reasonably good explanation of the economic
aspects of historical Norwegian demographic developments I set out to
explain, and on several specific points regarding historical economic-
demographic interactions my empirical conclusions differed from those
of previous studies. The reasons for this were reviewed in some detail
above and will not be repeated here. Rather, I will proceed to briefly
sketch some possibilities for further research in view of these findings
and the general limitations of this study.

VI-1. Additional Empirical Applications

One rather obvious extension of the above work would be to apply
the birth, marriage and migration models to a larger sample of nations.
The simple pre-emigration birth and marriage models could conceivably be
confronted with pre-industrial Swedish data for an independent test of
the conclusions reached in Chapter III. Similarly, it might be revealing
to test the investment hypothesis regarding historical overseas emigration on several of the individual countries from which emigrants sailed
for America in those years. This would not only throw additional light

on the general validity of the model as such, but also on several of the specific hypotheses entertained in this study and in the literature generally. Was, for example, the strong "push" effect regarding the timing of overseas departures a phenomenon peculiar to Scandinavian emigration? If so, why? To what extent did income differences and cohort effects, stemming in turn from prior cycles in births and emigration, combine to determine the trend and long swings in emigration from other countries? If nothing else, I will argue that the work on historical emigration carried out in this study points to several reasons why Professor Easterlin's work [A13] on aggregate immigration should be complemented by research on the individual country level. Aside from the fact that historical economic data now is much better than when he carried out his study 10 years ago, the empirical findings of the present paper revealed several important differences from his general conclusions. These may be due not only to differences in methodology, a point that was belabored at some length in Chapter V, but also to the possible differences entailed in studies of overseas emigration at different levels of aggregation.

Another possibility is to apply elements of the above econometric models to different time periods in Norwegian economic history. For example, to what extent does the pre-industrial birth model which was applied to a closed, pre-industrial economy have to be modified in light of the heavy overseas emigration stream that followed or, for that matter, the onset of industrialization in Norway? Research on this topic is presently being carried out by the author. Furthermore, what is the predictive power of a similar economic model of migration in explaining the extensive inter-

nal migration that has taken place in Norway after World War II? These
and similar questions suggest amendments and improvements in the models
themselves to which I now briefly turn.

VI-2. Further Research on Models of
Economic-Demographic Interactions

There are, I am sure, many limitations and short-comings contained in the present study. Some of these were explicitly set forth at
the outset. For example, economic factors were generally assumed to be
exogenously determined, and the well-known econometric implications of
the possible invalidity of such an assumption regarding the estimated
regression parameters have already been discussed. Thus one immediate
suggestion for further research would be to include some of the above
migration equations in the construction of a larger macro-economic model
of Norwegian historical economic growth. This possibility has been mentioned at several points in the dissertation. In such a model the emigration variable would presumably enter the equations determining the
aggregate supply of labor and the demand for "population sensitive" capital as one of several explanatory variables. In addition to exploring
some of the more general feedback effects of emigration on the variations
in demographic and economic variables that such a macro-model would allow, it would have the additional advantage of providing a framework for
rigorous tests of the long swing hypothesis of historical economic growth
which was briefly sketched in Chapter II. That is, one could use such a

model in an attempt to simulate the historical swings in aggregate output, investments and labor supply.

This may, indeed, be one general direction that research on economic-demographic interaction may go. A case in point is Professor Lebergott's work on participation rates and marriage rates as endogenous variables in the Brookings econometric model. See [B43]. Another very promising lead has been opened up by the recent work of Warren Sanderson, who has constructed disaggregated models of post-industrial fertility. See [A32a]. The relevance of such newly emerging work is obvious if one wants to extend the above models to more recent time periods.

Yet another element that may warrant closer consideration in further work on demographic phenomena is a closer look at other, strictly non-economic, factors. The sociological literature on migration is a case in point. That is to say, ideally one should not only work on a disaggregated level and construct models where both demographic and economic factors are assumed to be endogenously determined, one should also draw on the insights of other social sciences than demography and economics. Further work on for example migration models is one area where a more integrated socio-economic approach may be both warranted and possible.

APPENDIX A

A Brief Description of the Sources of the Empirical Data
used in the Regression Analysis of Chapter III

In the following I will limit myself to a brief description of the
empirical data employed in the regression analyses carried out in Chapter III. Whenever the data was taken directly from publications of historical statistics, these are simply given as data sources. However, when
the figures were created from the available primary statistical material,
I have, in addition, described the underlying assumptions made and the
methods employed.

(1) Births, Bt.   1801-1865 : [B14], Table 2, pp. 171-173.

(2) Marriages, Mt.   1801-1845 : [B14], Table 4, pp. 182-183.
           1846-1855 : [G1], Table 2, p. III.
           1856-1865 : [G2], Table 2, p. 34.

(3) The Stock of   1801-1845 : For this period I constructed yearly
Females, SFt.   figures of the stock of females between the ages
           20 and 49 from three primary statistical sources.
           The appropriate birth figures were taken, once more,
           from Drake, op. cit.
           Yearly data on age-specific female mortality was
           taken from [G2], Table No. 13, p. 204 and applied to
           the appropriate birth cohorts. Finally I checked
           these figures against the female age-structure data

found in [G2], Table No. 20, pp. 236-237. For the time period 1846-1865 the data was taken directly from [G8], Table 2, pp. 34-35.

(4) The Stock of Married and Unmarried Females, SMF and SUMF.

1801-1865 : Separate mortality figures for married females do not, to the best of my knowledge, exist. I was therefore forced to use the census figures on females distributed by age and marital condition. Source: [G2], Table No. 20, pp. 236-237. Between census dates I arrived at yearly figures by linear interpolations of the yearly SF figures.

(5) Dummy Variables.

1801-1845 : Qualitative descriptions of exceptional years were taken from the following sources: [B64], pp. 24-30, [B3], pp. 48-55 and, in addition, O. Klokk: Oversigt over det norske landbruks utvikling siden 1750 (Survey of the Development of Norwegian Agriculture after 1750). Kristiania: Erichsen et Co., 1920, pp. 30-31.

In model (3.2.3) the following dummy variables were employed:

d   : 1809, 1811, 1812, 1817, 1839

dd : 1813, 1814

c   : 1815, 1820, 1825, 1826, 1829, 1830, 1833, 1834, 1835.

The general criteria for entering the dummy variables were that I required some concensus from the three different authors. If all three, or two without being contradicted by the third writer, characterized a year as one of abundant or especially deficient harvest, I entered c's and d's respectively. However, if one researcher contradicted another, as for example was the case for the year 1810, no dummy variable was entered. The justification for entering dd in 1813 and 1814, as distinct from d's in other deficient harvest years, was given at some length in the text in Chapter III.

1846-1865. In model (3.3.5) I entered dummy variables in 1846, 1854 and 1855. The justification for this is based on the description of the economic fluctuations of this period in [B31], p. 60 and pp. 65-68.

(6) Economic Condition, EC.

1846-1865 : The index refers to the number of relief recipients per 1000 of population. For the period 1851-1865 the data is taken directly from [G3], Table No. 13, p. 23.

For the period 1846-1850 this series was extrapolated backwards on the basis of quantity series of imports and exports taken from [G16], Table 117, pp. 190-192 and Table 120, pp. 205-206.

The reason for chosing this index from very limited
number of series was that this is the primary statistical material underlying the unemployment figures
after 1865. It is obvious that it is, at best, a very
crude index of "unemployment" although lack of employment was the criteria used for relief payments. The
series is probably insensitive to major crisis or
boom periods, but I found it preferable to the trade
series since one lacks price data on exports and imports. In addition the import and export quantities
exhibit pronounced trends over the twenty year period,
and I did not in addition want to get involved in the
vagaries of trend removal which is, at best, a very
tricky business.

(7) Grain Prices.   For the period 1820-1835 I adapted the data given in
T. H. Aschehoug: "Studier over kornprisernes historie
siden Amerikas oppdagelse" (Studies of the Development
of Grain Prices since the Discovery of America). Stats-
ökonomisk Tidskrift, 1888, pp. 81-116, as closely as
I could to the yearly data for the post-1836 period
published in [G10]. For the period 1836-1865 the data
was taken directly from [G10], pp. 3-4.

APPENDIX B

A Brief Description of the Data Used in the
Regression Analyses of Chapter V

In section 1 below I briefly set forth the empirical material underlying the regression work in Chapter V above. In section 2 I have made
an attempt at comparing the available relevant wage data in the U.S. and
Norway before World War I. While especially the Norwegian wage data allegedly is of poor quality, this comparison may have some interest in that
it verifies the contention that earnings differences in the two regions
were marked during the period of mass Norwegian overseas emigration. While
yearly Norwegian wage-data is largely unavailable, a comparison of the wage
data with the labor productivity data that was used as a proxy variable
in the regression analyses at bench-mark years shows that labor productivity
differences seem to be a reasonable proxy for the earnings differences
that existed at the time.

1. Data used in the regression analysis

in Chapter V

1.1. Dependent variable, Mt

The age and sex distribution of Norwegian overseas emigrants for each
year was taken from yearly publications of The Movement of Population from
the Norwegian Central Bureau of Statistics (N.C.B.S.) each year 1873-1914.
The percentage of Norwegian overseas emigrants that traveled to the United
States was computed from [B19], Table IV, p. 752. Since this percentage

refers to the total number of emigrants, it was assumed that this percentage did not vary between age groups. Thus it was applied to the total
number of overseas emigrants between 15 and 44 years of age to arrive at
the total number of migrants in this age group that traveled to the U.S.
Since the number lies between 95 and 100 for the entire period, no large
bias is likely to occur because of this assumption. Finally, the absolute
number of emigrants between 15 and 44 that traveled to the U.S. was expressed as a rate per 1000 of mean Norwegian population in this age-group
which in turn was computed from the data given in [G8].

1.2. Independent variable PY

A five year moving average of U.S. national product per member of
labor force (in 1929 prices) was available directly from [B42], Table R-40,
pp. 633-34, col. 4. Norwegian national product was taken from [B6], Table
XIII, p. 130, col. 7, and [G18], Table 16, p. 132, col. 7. Yearly data on
the Norwegian labor force was obtained from unpublished material kindly
provided by researcher Juul Bjerke at N.C.B.S., and the yearly figures of
Norwegian national product per member of labor force were computed and
smoothed by a five year moving average. The difference between the U.S.
and Norwegian moving averages could then be obtained by centering the respective series on the same year after the Norwegian figure had been converted into "dollar-equivalents" by multiplying it by the official exchange
rate. The units therefore become the real U.S. GNP/L minus the Norwegian
real GNP/L in dollar "equivalents".

1.3. Independent variable EUS

The proxy used for yearly employment conditions in the U.S. was Frickey's trend adjusted index of production for transportation and communication. Source [B22], Table 18, p. 119. The units of measurement refer to the yearly standing of the index as a percent of its trend which is represented by a fitted logarithmic parabola. The resulting percentages were compared with Lebergott's estimates of the percent of the labor force unemployed in the years of "economic crisis" up to 1890, and his yearly data for the period 1890 to 1914. See [B44], Table 4-3, p. 187, and Table 2-2, p. 43 respectively. The peaks and troughs in the two series are almost identical for the entire period.

Furthermore, when one compares the yearly data of both these series as measured in units of standard deviation between 1890 and 1914, they move almost synchronously during the 25 years when both are available. See Chart B-1. As seen from this chart, the unemployment series move in the same direction as the (inverted) Frickey index in 23 out of the 25 years. I.e., sign tests show that the production index (inverted) shows the same direction of movement in 23 out of the 25 cases exhibited in this chart. The Pearsonian or product movement coefficient of correlation between Frickey's index and Lebergott's unemployment figures was computed on the basis of yearly data and found to be equal to -0.833, which indicates a highly statistically significant relationship between the two series. It was therefore concluded that Frickey's yearly index numbers would be a reasonable proxy for year to year movements in the U.S. labor market before World War I.

CHART B-1

A COMPARISON OF FRICKEY'S PRODUCTION INDEX AND LEBERGOTT'S
YEARLY UNEMPLOYMENT FIGURES 1890-1914

Both series are in units of standard deviation.

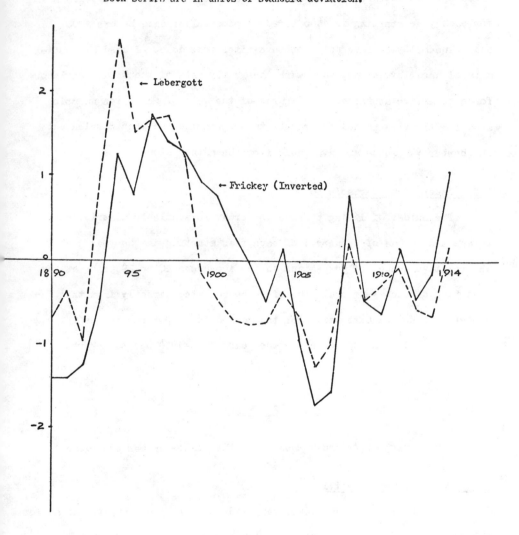

1.4. Independent variable UN

Juul Bjerke at the Norwegian Central Bureau of Statistics has estimated the absolute number of unemployed economically active Norwegians
for each year starting in 1866 based on poor relief data before 1900
and on unemployed trade union members after this date. I used his estimate of unemployment together with the yearly data of the Norwegian labor
force to arrive at the yearly figures of the rate of Norwegian unemployment for the time period covered by the regression analyses carried out
in Chapter V. These are available from the author upon request.

1.5. Independent variable CO

The number of living persons in Norway is available distributed as
to age and sex as of January 1 of each year starting in the year 1846.
The relative number of Norwegians in the age-group 20 to 29 years at the
beginning of each year could therefore be computed directly from this
demographic source material. For the period 1873-1901 the source is [G8],
1901-1911 [G11], and the data for the years 1911-1914 was taken from [G14].

2. Wages

In arriving at Appendix Table B-1, the following was considered:

2.1. Occupations and skill

It is well known that wages vary widely as to the occupational and/or
skill mix of the employee. Since a high percentage of the Norwegian emigrants were relatively unskilled (rural) laborers, this category was sin-
gled out for comparison.

2.2. Regional wage differentials in the U.S.

Since wages varied between U.S. regions, the regions to which Norwegians typically migrated were considered. During the 1870's and 1880's
they settled in the East and West North Central regions, in the 1890's and
the first decade of the 20th century a large percentage traveled to the
West North Central and Pacific regions. See also Table IV-3 in the text.

2.3. Monthly versus daily wages

Lebergott advises us that: "For most of the nineteenth century and
well into the twentieth, the common method of wage payment in agriculture
was monthly with board included." [B44], p. 257. To make Norwegian daily
wage data (monthly data is not available) for rural labor with board comparable to Lebergott's data on average monthly earnings of farm labor,
these were simply multiplied by 26. This, however, may have induced a
certain bias, because historically in the U.S. there generally was a gap
between monthly payments and daily payments because: "the prospect of constant employment was much more durable for jobs by the month than by the
day." ibid., p. 244. There is no reason to believe that this was not true
for Scandinavia as well, so that daily wages times 26 will be an overesti-
mate of monthly wages. As a check on the monthly ratios therefore, the
ratio of daily wages of rural common laborers (without board) in both regions was computed. For our purposes the ratios are not too dissimilar,
compare lines 1-3 with lines 4-6 in Table B-1.

2.4. Money versus real wages. Kroner versus dollars

For the wage data that includes board, the reported money wages were

APPENDIX TABLE B-1

NORWEGIAN WAGES OF UNSKILLED RURAL LABOR RELATIVE TO U.S. U.S. = 100

	YEAR	1850	1860	1870	1880	1890	1899	1909
Norwegian average monthly rural labor wage with board relative to average farm labor wage with board, East North Central region	1	29.2	32.3	30.4	41.0	45.5	56.5	53.5
Norwegian average monthly rural labor wage with board relative to average monthly earnings of farm labor with board, West North Central region	2	27.9	32.4	30.2	42.6	46.8	52.9	47.6
Norwegian average monthly rural labor wage with board relative to the average monthly earnings of farm labor with board, Pacific region	3				25.6	32.0	38.0	36.8
Average daily real earnings Norwegian common rural labor without board as a percent of average real daily earnings rural labor without board, East North Central region	4			36.7	51.3	47.2		
Average daily real earnings Norwegian common rural labor without board as a percent of average real daily earnings without rural labor board, West North Central region	5			37.4	46.5	48.0		
Average daily real earnings Norwegian common rural labor without board as a percent of average real daily earnings without board, Pacific region	6					36.4		
Norwegian real daily rural wage of common labor as a percent of real daily urban wage in Norway	7			85.8	71.7	82.0	81.6	80.7

Sources: i) Norwegian money wages [G16], Table 193, p. 366

ii) U.S. money wages [B44], Tables A-23, A-24, A-25, pp. 539-541

iii) Norwegian consumer price index [B6], Table XVII, p. 142, col. 2   1910 = 100
[G18], Table 13, p. 127, col. 2

iv) U.S. consumer price index [B50], Table B-1, B-2, App. B, pp. 156-157
[B59], Table 1, p. 4   1914 = 100

used. For the (daily) wage data that excludes board, the money wages were deflated by consumer price indexes where 1910 = 100. To convert Norwegian kroner into U.S. dollars, the (constant) official exchange rate for the entire period was used where $1.00 = kr. 3.73. This is of course crude, but no alternative seemed available.

The resulting figures are reasonably consistent with the hypothesis that a clear wage differential existed between the two regions during the period under analysis, the U.S. wage being from two to three times as large as the one obtainable in the region of departure. Furthermore, it is unlikely that the use of the exchange rate factor between the two currencies will introduce a bias large enough to make a comparison between lines 1-6 (rural wages Norway vs. U.S.) and line 7 (rural-urban wages in Norway) meaningless. Thus, given employment opportunities, the gain in income that a potential rural migrant could obtain by traveling to the U.S. was substantial and higher than the gain obtainable by migrating to a Norwegian city. Since the cost of living in urban areas allegedly is 10 to 15 percent above the rural equivalent (no data, to the best of my knowledge, exist for the period to quantify this rough estimate exactly), the urban-rural wage differential for unskilled labor probably overestimates the real income gain available to an urban migrant in this category. This adds some support to the above contention. A pecuniary gain hypothesis seems therefore to be a relatively reasonable starting point for an analysis of Norwegian emigration to the U.S. before World War I.

Furthermore, if one compares the above wage data with the average labor productivity figures that were used in the regression analyses in Chapter 5 at bench-mark years, one finds that the movement in the two series is very similar. Hopefully, then, one is not too far off the mark in using labor productivity differences as a proxy for wage differences in the analytical work attempted in that chapter.

BIBLIOGRAPHY

Series A: Articles

A1 Abramovitz, M.   "The Nature and Significance of Kuznets Cycles"
                      Economic Development and Cultural Change,
                      Vol. IX, No. 3 (April, 1961), pp. 225-248.
                      Reprinted in Gordon and Klein ed. Readings in
                      Business Cycles, Chp. 27. London: G. Allen
                      Unwin Ltd, 1966.

A2 _____   "The Passing of the Kuznets Cycle"
                      Economica, Vol. XXXV, No. 140 (November, 1968),
                      pp. 349-367.

A3 Adelman, I.   "An Econometric Analysis of Population Growth"
                      American Economic Review. Vol. LIII, No. 3
                      (June 1963), pp. 314-339.

A4 _____   "Long Cycles — Fact or Artifact?"
                      American Economic Review, Vol. LV, No. 3 (June
                      1965), pp. 444-463.

A5 Barca, P.   "Development of the Norwegian Agricultural
                      Statistics"
                      Articles No. 5. N.C.B.S., Oslo, 1958.

A6 Becker, G. S.   "Investment in Human Capital: A Theoretical
                      Analysis"
                      Journal of Political Economy, Vol. LXX, No. 5,
                      Part 2 (Oct. 1962), pp. 9-49.

A7 Blacker, C. P.   "Stages in Population Growth"
                      Eugenics Review, Vol. XXXIX, 1947, pp. 88-101.

A8 Campbell, B. O.   "Long Swings in Residental Construction: The
                      Postwar Experience"
                      American Economic Review, Vol. LIII, No. 2 (May
                      1963), pp. 506-512.

A9 Chow, G. C.   "Test of Equality between Sets of Coefficients
                      in Two Linear Regressions"
                      Econometrica, Vol. 28, No. 3 (July 1960),
                      pp. 591-605.

A10 Davis, K.   "Theory of Change and Response in Modern Demo-
                      graphic History"
                      Population Index, Vol. 29, 1963, pp. 345-366.

A11 Drake, M.

"The Growth of Population in Norway 1735-1855"
Scandinavian Economic History Review, Vol. XIII,
No. 2, 1965, pp. 97-142.

A12 Durbin, J. and
Watson, G. S.

"Testing for Serial Correlation in Least Squares
Regression"
Biometrika, Part I: Vol. XXXVII, 1950, pp. 409-
429, Part II: Vol. XXXVIII, 1951, pp. 159-178.

A13 Easterlin, R. E.

"Influences in European Overseas Emigration Before
World War I"
Economic Development and Cultural Change, Vol. IX,
No. 3 (April 1961), pp. 331-351.

A14 ———————————

"Economic-Demographic Interactions and Long
Swings in Economic Growth"
American Economic Review, Vol. LVI, No. 5 (De-
cember 1966), pp. 1063-1104.

A15 Gille, H.

"The Demographic History of the Northern European Countries in the Eighteenth Century"
Population Studies, Vol. III, Part I (June 1949),
pp. 3-65.

A16 Griliches, Z.

"Distributed Lags: A Survey"
Econometrica, Vol. 35, No. 1 (January 1967),
pp. 16-49.

A17 Habakkuk, H. J.

"English Population in the Eighteenth Century"
Economic History Review, 2nd Series, Vol. VI,
1953, pp. 117-133.
Reprinted in Glass and Eversley ed. Population
in History. Essays in Historical Demography.
Chicago: Aldine Pub. Co, 1965.

A18 Hahn, F. H. and
Matthews, R. C. O.

"The Theory of Economic Growth: A Survey"
Economic Journal, Vol. LXXIC, No. 296 (December
1964), pp. 779-902.
Reprinted in: Surveys of Economic Theory, Vol. II,
Growth and Development, Essay V. New York:
St. Martin's Press, 1967.

A19 Heckscher, E. F.

"Swedish Population Trends Before the Industrial
Revolution"
Economic History Review, 2nd Series, Vol. II,
No. 2 (1950), pp. 266-277.

A20 Kelley, A. C.   "International Migration and Economic Growth: Australia, 1865-1935" *Journal of Economic History*, Vol. XXV, No. 3 (September 1965), pp. 333-354.

A21 ─────────── "Demographic Cycles and Economic Growth: The Long Swing Reconsidered" *Journal of Economic History*, Vol. XXIX, No. 4 (December 1969), pp. 633-656.

A22 Kelley, A. C. and Weiss, L. W.   "Markov Processes and Economic Analysis: The Case of Migration" *Econometrica*, Vol. 37, No. 2 (April 1969), pp. 280-297.

A23 Lettenström, G. S. and Skancke, G.   "The Economically Active Population in Norway 1875-1960 and Forcasts up to 1970" *Articles No. 10*, N.C.B.S., Oslo, 1964.

A24 Lettenström, G. S.   "Marriages and Number of Children — An Analysis of Fertility Trend in Norway" *Articles No. 14*, N.C.B.S., Oslo, 1965.

A25 Levine, A. L.   "Economic Science and Population Theory" *Population Studies*, Vol. XIX, No. 2 (November 1965), pp. 139-154.

A26 Lewis, J. P.   "Growth and Inverse Cycles: A Two-Country Model" *Economic Journal*, Vol. LXXIV, No. 293 (March 1964), pp. 109-118.

A27 Lösch, A.   "Population Cycles as a Cause of Business Cycles" *Quarterly Journal of Economics*, Vol. LI (August 1937), pp. 649-662.

A28 Mendels, F. F.   "Population Pressure and Rural Industrialization in Early Modern Europe" Paper given at the Purdue Economic History Conference January, 1969.

A28a Moe, T.   "Some Economic Aspects of Norwegian Population Movements 1740-1940: An Econometric Analysis" *The Journal of Economic History*, Vol. XXX, No. 1 (March 1970), pp. 267-70.

A29 Nelson, P.   "Migration, Real Income and Information" *Journal of Regional Science*, Vol. 1, No. 2 (Spring 1959), pp. 43-73.

A30 Nelson, R. R. "A Theory of the Low-Level Equilibrium Trap in Underdeveloped Economies" _American Economic Review_, Vol. XLVI, No. 5 (December 1956), pp. 894-908.

A31 Nerlove, M. and Wallis, K. F. "Use of the Durbin-Watson Statistic in Inappropriate Situations" _Econometrica_, Vol. 34, No.1 (January 1966), pp. 235-238.

A32 Reder, M. W. "The Economic Consequences of Increased Immigration" _Review of Economics and Statistics_, Vol. XLV, No. 3 (August 1963), pp. 221-230.

A32a Sanderson, W. "The Fertility of American Women Since 1920" _The Journal of Economic History_, Vol. XXX, No. 1 (March 1970), pp. 271-272.

A33 Silver, M. "Births, Marriages, and Business Cycles in the United States" _Journal of Political Economy_, Vol. LXXIII, No. 3 (June 1965), pp. 237-255.

A34 Sjaastad, L. A. "The Costs and Returns of Human Migration" _Journal of Political Economy_, Vol. LXX, No. 5, Part 2 (October 1962), pp. 80-93.

A35 Solow, R. M. "A Contribution to the Theory of Economic Growth" _Quarterly Journal of Economics_, Vol. 70 (February 1956), pp. 65-94.

A36 Soltow, L. "Evidence on Income Equality in the United States" _Journal of Economic History_, Vol. XXIV, No. 2 (June 1969), pp. 279-286.

A37 Theil, H. "Specification Errors and the Estimation of Economic Relationships" _Review International Statistical Institute_, Vol. 25 (1957), pp. 41-51.

A38 Todaro, M. P. "A Model of Labor Migration and Urban Unemployment in Less Developed Countries" _American Economic Review_, Vol. LIX, No. 1 (March 1969), pp. 138-148.

A39 Utterström, G. "Some Population Problems in Pre-Industrial Sweden" _Scandinavian Economic History Review_, Vol. II, No. 1 (1954), pp. 103-165.

A40   Vogt, J.   "Component Parts of the Number of Births"
                               Statsökonomisk Tidsskrift, No. 4 (1964), pp. 287-
                               307.

A41   Wallis, K. F.   "Some Recent Developments in Applied Econometrics:
                               Dynamic Models and Simultaneous Equation Systems"
                               Journal of Economic Literature, Vol. VII, No. 3
                               (September 1969), pp. 771-796.

A42   Weintraub, R.   "The Birth Rate and Economic Development: An Em-
                               pirical Study"
                               Econometrica, Vol. 40, No. 4 (October 1962),
                               pp. 812-817.

A43   Wilkinson, M.   "Evidences of Long Swings in the Growth of Swedish
                               Population and Related Economic Variables, 1860-
                               1965"
                               Journal of Economic History, Vol. XXVII, No. 1
                               (March 1967), pp. 17-30.

Series B: Books, Chapters in Books and Memoranda

B1 Aukrust, O. ed.   The Norwegian Post-War Economy. S.Ø.S. No. 12.
                           Oslo: N.C.B.S., 1965.

B2 Backer, J. E.   Trend of Mortality and Causes of Death in Norway,
                           1856-1955. S.Ø.S. No. 10. Oslo: N.C.B.S., 1961.

B3 ——————————   Marriages, Births and Migrations in Norway, 1856-
                           1960. S.Ø.S. No. 13. Oslo: N.C.B.S., 1965.

B4 Becker, G. S.   "An Economic Analysis of Fertility" in: Demo-
                           graphic and Economic Change in Developed Coun-
                           tries, pp. 209-231. N.B.E.R. Special Conference
                           Series, No. 11. Princeton: Princeton Univ.
                           Press, 1960.

B5 ——————————   Human Capital. A Theoretical and Empirical Anal-
                           ysis, with Special Reference to Education.
                           N.B.E.R. No. 80, General Series. New York:
                           Columbia Univ. Press, 1964.

B6 Bjerke, J.   Trends in the Norwegian Economy 1865-1960. S.Ø.S.
                           No. 16. Oslo: N.C.B.S., 1966.

B7 Bjork, K. O.   West of the Great Divide. Norwegian Migration to
                           the Pacific Coast, 1847-1893. Norwegian-American
                           Historical Association. Northfield, Minnesota,
                           1958.

B8 Blegen, T. C.   Norwegian Migration to America, 1825-1860. Nor-
                           wegian-American Historical Association. North-
                           field, Minnesota, 1931.

B9 Bull, E.   "Industrialization as a Factor in Economic Growth.
                           Norway" In: First International Conference of
                           Economic History, pp. 261-272. Paris: Mouton Co.,
                           1960.

B10 Campbell, B. O.   Population Change and Building Cycles. Urbana,
                           Illinois, 1961.

B11 Carpenter, N.   Immigrants and Their Children, 1920. Census Mono-
                           graphs VII. Dep. of Commerce, Bureau of the Cen-
                           sus. Washington, 1927.

B12 Christ, C. F.   Econometric Models and Methods. New York: John
                           Wiley and Sons Inc., 1966.

B13   Denison, E. F.   "Comment" in: <u>Trends in the American Economy in</u>
<u>the Nineteenth Century</u>. N.B.E.R. Studies in
Income and Wealth, Vol. 24. Princeton: Princeton
Univ. Press, 1961.

B14   Drake, M.   <u>Population and Society in Norway 1735-1865</u>. Cambridge: Cambridge Univ. Press, 1969.

B15   Easterlin, R. A.   "Regional Income Trends, 1840-1950" in: Harris
ed. <u>American Economic History</u>, Chp. 16, pp. 525-
547. New York: McGraw-Hill, 1961.

B16   —————————   <u>Population, Labor Force, and Long Swings in Eco-</u>
<u>nomic Growth. The American Experience</u>. N.B.E.R.
No. 86, General Series. New York: Columbia Univ.
Press, 1968.

B17   Erickson, C.   <u>American Industry and the European Immigrant,</u>
<u>1860-1885</u>. Cambridge, Mass.: Harvard Univ.
Press, 1957.

B18   Eversley, D. E. C.   "Population, Economy and Society" in: Glass and
Eversley ed.: <u>Population in History. Essays in</u>
<u>Historical Demography"</u>. Chicago: Aldine Pub.
Co., 1965.

B19   Ferenczi, I.   <u>International Migrations. Vol. I. Statistics.</u>
N.E.B.R. Inc. New York, 1929.

B20   Fishlow, A.   <u>American Railroads and the Transformation of the</u>
<u>Ante-Bellum Economy</u>. Cambridge, Mass.: Harvard
Univ. Press, 1964.

B21   Flom, G. T.   <u>A History of Norwegian Immigration to the United</u>
<u>States</u>. Iowa,City, Iowa, 1909.

B22   Frickey, E.   <u>Production in The United States 1860-1914</u>.
Cambridge, Mass.: Harvard Univ. Press, 1947.

B23   Gallman, R. E.   "Trends in the Size Distribution of Wealth in
the Nineteenth Century: Some Speculations" in:
Soltow, L. ed. <u>Six Papers on the Size Distribu-</u>
<u>tion of Wealth and Income</u>. N.B.E.R. Studies in
Income and Wealth, Vol. 33. New York: Columbia
Univ. Press, 1969.

B24   Glass, D. V. and
      Eversley, D. E. C.
      ed.   <u>Population in History. Essays in Historical</u>
<u>Demography</u>. Chicago: Aldine Pub. Co., 1965.

B25 Goldberger, A. S.   Topics in Regression Analysis. New York: The
                           Macmillan Co., 1968.

B26 Haavelmo, T.   A Study in the Theory of Economic Evolution.
                           Amsterdam: North-Holland Pub. Co., 1954.

B27 Himes, N. E.   Medical History of Contraception. Baltimore:
                           The Williams and Wilkins Co., 1936.

B28 Hoem, J. M.   Grunnbegreper i formell befolkningslære (Basic
                           Concepts in Formal Demography). Memorandum
                           from The Institute of Economics at the Univ. of
                           Oslo, February 7, 1967.

B29 Hutchinson, E. P.   Immigrants and Their Children, 1850-1950. A vol-
                           ume in the Census Monograph Series. New York:
                           J. Wiley, 1956.

B30 Isaac, J.   Economics of Migration. Oxford: Oxford Univ.
                           Press, 1947.

B31 Jahn, G.   Norges Bank Gjennom 150 År (The History of the
                           Bank of Norway 1016-1966). Oslo, 1966.

B32 Jerome, H.   Migration and Business Cycles. N.B.E.R. Inc.
                           New York, 1926.

B33 Johansen, L.   A Multi-Sectoral Study of Economic Growth.
                           Amsterdam: North-Holland Pub. Co., 1964.

B34 Johnston, J.   Econometric Methods. New York: McGraw-Hill
                           Book Co., Inc., 1963.

B35 Kendall, M. G. and   The Advanced Theory of Statistics. Vol. 2.
     Stuart, A.   Inference and Relationship. London: C. Griffin
                           and Co. Ltd., 1961.

B36 Keyfitz, N.   Introduction To The Mathematics of Population.
                           Reading, Mass.: Addison-Wesley Pub. Co., 1968.

B37 Kirk, D.   "The Influence of Business Cycles on Marriage
                           and Birth Rates" in Demographic and Economic
                           Change in Developed Countries, pp. 241-260.
                           N.B.E.R. Special Conference Series, No. 11.
                           Princeton: Princeton Univ. Press, 1960.

B38 Kiær, A. N.   Nye Bidrag til Belysning af Frugtbarheds For-
                           holdene inden Ægteskabet, Norge (An Analysis of
                           Marrital Fertility in Norway). Videnskabssel-
                           skabets Skrifter II. Historisk-Filosofisk
                           Klasse. No. 3. Christiania, 1902.

B39   Koyck, L. M.   Distributed Lags and Investment Analysis. Amsterdam: North-Holland Pub. Co., 1954.

B40   Kuznets, S. and Rubin, E.   Immigration and the Foreign Born. Occasional Paper No. 46, N.B.E.R., 1954.

B41   Kuznets, S., Miller, A. R. and Easterlin, R. A.   Population Redistribution and Economic Growth, United States, 1870-1950. Vol II. Analyses of Economic Change. Philadelphia: The American Philosophical Society, 1960.

B42   Kuznets, S.   Capital in the American Economy. Its Formation and Financing. N.B.E.R. Studies in Capital Formation and Financing, No. 9. Princeton Univ. Press, 1961.

B43   Lebergott, S.   "The Labor Force and Marriages as Endogenous Factors" in: Dusenberry, J. S., Fromm, G., Klein, L. R., Kuh, E. ed.: The Brookings Quarterly Econometric Model of the United States. Chp. 10, pp. 335-371. Chicago: Rand McNally Co., 1965.

B44   ————————   Manpower in Economic Growth. The United States Record since 1800. New York: McGraw-Hill Book Co., 1964.

B45   Lee, E. S., Brainerd, C. P., Miller, A. R., Easterlin, R. A.   Population Redistribution and Economic Growth, United States, 1870-1950. Vol I. Philadelphia: The American Philosophical Society, 1957.

B46   Leibenstein, H.   A Theory of Economic-Demographic Development. Princeton: Princeton Univ. Press, 1954.

B47   ————————   Economic Backwardness and Economic Growth. New York: J. Wiley and Sons Inc., Science Editions, 1963.

B48   Lewis, J. P.   Building Cycles and Britain's Growth. New York: St. Martin's Press, 1965.

B49   Lieberman, S.   The Industrialization of Norway: 1800-1920. Oslo: Oslo Univ. Press, 1970.

B50   Long, C. D.   Wages and Earnings in the United States 1860-1890. N.B.E.R. No. 67, General Series. Princeton: Princeton Univ. Press, 1961.

B51   Lösch, A.   Bevölkerungswellen und Wechsellagen. Jena: Verlag von G. Fischer, 1936.

B52 Matthews, R. C. O.   The Business Cycle. Chicago: Chicago Univ.
                           Press, 1959.

B53 Myklebost, H.   Norges Tettbyrde Steder 1875-1950 (Urban Settle-
                           ments in Norway 1875-1950). Oslo: Oslo Univ.
                           Press, 1960.

B54 North, D. C.   The Economic Growth of the United States 1790-
                           1860. Englewood Cliffs, N.J.: Prentice Hall,
                           Inc., 1961.

B55 Ohlin, P. G.   Positive and Preventive Checks: A Study of the
                           Rate of Growth of a Pre-Industrial Population.
                           Unpublished Harvard University Ph.D. disserta-
                           tion, 1956.

B56 Parzen, E.   Stochastic Processes. San Francisco: Holden-
                           Day, 1962.

B57 Qualey, C.   Norwegian Settlement in the United States. Nor-
                           wegian American Historical Association, North-
                           field, Minnesota, 1938.

B58 Reder, M. W.   Labor in a Growing Economy. New York: J. Wiley
                           and Sons Inc.. 1957.

B59 Rees, A.   Real Wages in Manufacturing 1890-1914. N.B.E.R.
                           No. 70, General Series. Princeton: Princeton
                           Univ. Press, 1961.

B60 Semmingsen, I.   Veien Mot Vest. Utvandringen Fra Norge til Amer-
                           ica, 1825-1865 (Norwegian Emigration to America
                           1825-1865). Oslo: Aschehough, 1941.

B61 ——————————   Veien Mot Vest. Utvandringen Fra Norge til Amer-
                           ica, 1865-1915 (Norwegian Emigration to America
                           1865-1915). Oslo: Aschehough, 1950.

B62 Skaug, A.   "Memorandum on fluctuations in migration from
                           Norway since 1900, compared with other countries
                           and causes of these fluctuations" in: Inter-
                           national Institute of Intellectual Co-operation.
                           Norwegian Memorandum No. 1, Paris, 1937.

B62a Soltow, L.   Toward Income Equality in Norway. Milwaukee:
                           The University of Wisconsin Press, 1965.

B63 Spengler, J. J.   "Effects Produced in Receiving Countries by Pre-1939 Immigration" in: Thomas, B. ed.: Economics of International Migration. Proceedings of a Conference held by the International Economic Association. New York: St. Martin's Press, 1958.

B64 Steen, S.   Det Gamle Samfunn (The Traditional Society). Oslo: Cappelen, 1957.

B65 Stonehill, A.   Foreign Ownership in Norwegian Enterprises. S.Ø.S. No. 14. Oslo: N.C.B.S., 1965.

B66 Sundt, E.   Om Giftermål i Norge (On Marriage in Norway). Oslo: Oslo Univ. Press, 2nd ed., 1967. First published in 1855.

B67 Thomas, B.   Migration and Economic Growth. London: Cambridge Univ. Press, 1954.

B68 ————   International Migration and Economic Development. A trend report and bibliography. Unesco, 1961.

B69 Thomas, D. S.   Social and Economic Aspects of Swedish Population Movements 1750-1933. New York: The Macmillan Co., 1941.

B70 ————   Social Aspects of the Business Cycle. Demographic Monographs, Vol. 1. New York: Gordon and Breach Science Pub., 1967. First published in 1927 by A. A. Knopf.

B71 Thomas, D. S. and Eldridge, H. T.   Population Redistribution and Economic Growth. United States 1870-1950. Vol. III. Philadelphia: The American Philosophical Society, 1964.

B72 Thomlinson, R.   Population Dynamics. Causes and Consequences of World Demographic Change. New York: Random House, 1965.

B73 Valen-Sendstad, F.   Norske Landbruksredskaper 1800-1850 årene (Norwegian Agricultural Tools 1800-1850). Lillehammer: De Sandvigske Samlinger, 1964.

B74 Vogt, J.   En Generasjonsstatistikk for det norske folk (Generation Statistics for the Norwegian Population). Memorandum from The Institute of Economics at the Univ. of Oslo, January 29, 1957.

Series G: Government Publications

Norwegian Publications. The following abbreviations will be used:
N.O.S. = Norwegian Official Statistics. N.C.B.S. = The Norwegian Central
Bureau of Statistics.

G1 Sextende Række,   indeholdene Tabeller over Folkemængden i Norge
                               den 31te December 1855 samt over de i tidsrum-
                               met 1846-1855 Ægteviede, Fødte og Døde (Data
                               on the Pop. Census 1855 and Movement of the
                               Population 1846-1855).
                               Dep. for det Indre, Christiania, 1857.

G2 C. No. 1   Tabeller vedkommende Folkemængdens Bevegelse i
                               Aarene 1856-1865 (Movement of Pop. 1856-1865).
                               Dep. for det Indre, Christiania 1869.

G3   Tabellarisk Fremstilling af Norges Økonomiske
                               Udvikling i Aarene 1851-1875 (tildels 1845-1876)
                               (Survey of Economic Developments in Norway 1845-
                               1876). N.C.B.S. Kristiania, 1878.

G4 C. No. 1   Resultaterne af Folketællingen i Norge 1. Januar
                               1876 (Norw. Pop. Census 1876).
                               N.C.B.S. Kristiania 1876-1881.

G5 N.O.S. III, No. 106   Folkemengdens Bevegelse 1866-1885. Hovedover-
                               sigt (Mov. of Norw. Pop. 1866-1885).
                               N.C.B.S. Kristiania, 1890.

G6 N.O.S. III, No. 259   Folkemængde fordelt efter livsstilling med an-
                               givelse av alder og egteskabelig stilling
                               1. januar 1891 (Norw. Pop. Census 1891).
                               N.C.B.S. Kristiania, 1897.

G7 N.O.S. IV, No. 73   2. hefte: Folkemængde fordelt efter kjønn, alder
                               og egteskaplig stilling 3/12, 1900 (Norw. Pop.
                               Census 1900, Vol. 2).
                               N.C.B.S. Kristiania, 1903.

G8 N.O.S. V, No. 113   Norges folkemængde 1846-1901 fordelt paa de
                               enkelte aldersaar (The Norw. Pop Distributed
                               by Age, 1846-1901).
                               N.C.B.S. Kristiania, 1910.

G9 N.O.S. VI, No. 8   5. hefte: Folkemængde fordelt efter kjøn, alder
                               og egteskabelig stilling samt fødesteder. Frem-
                               mede staters undersaatter (Norw. Pop. Census
                               1910, Vol. 5). N.C.B.S. Kristiania, 1914.

G10 N.O.S. VI, No. 23   Markedspriser paa korn og poteter 1836-1914
(Market prices of grain and potatoes 1836-1914).
N.C.B.S. Kristiania, 1915.

G11 N.O.S. VI, No. 45   Dødlighetstabeller for det norske folk 1901/02-
1910/11 (Mortality Tables Norw. Pop. 1901/02-
1910/11). N.C.B.S. Kristiania, 1915.

G12   Statistiske Oversigter 1914 (Statistical Survey
1914). N.C.B.S. Kristiania, 1914.

G13 N.O.S. VII, No. 25   Utvandringsstatistikk (Emigration Statistics).
N.C.B.S. Kristiania, 1921.

G14 N.O.S. VII, No. 142   Dødlighetstabeller for det norske folk 1911/12-
1920/21 (Norw. Mortality Tables 1911/12-1920/21)
N.C.B.S. Oslo, 1924.

G15 N.O.S. IX, No. 36   Dødlighetstabeller for det norske folk 1921/22-
1930/31 (Norw. Mortality Tables 1921/22-1930/31)
N.C.B.S. Oslo, 1934.

G16 N.O.S. X, No. 178   Statistiske Oversikter 1948 (Statistical Survey
1948). N.C.B.S. Oslo, 1949.

G17 N.O.S. XI, No. 113   Sosialstatistikkens historie i Norge gjennom
100 år (1850-1950) (The History of Social Sta-
tistics in Norway during 100 years 1850-1950).
N.C.B.S. Oslo, 1952.

G18 N.O.S. XI, No. 143   Nasjonalregnskap 1900-1929 (National Accounts
1900-1929). N.C.B.S. Oslo, 1953.

G19 N.O.S. XII, No. 163   Nasjonalregnskap 1865-1960 (National Accounts
1865-1960). N.C.B.S. Oslo, 1965.

G20 N.O.S. XII, No. 245   Historisk Statistikk 1968 (Historical Statistics
1968). N.C.B.S. Oslo, 1969.

G21 Oslo County   Statistical Yearbook 1925. Oslo, 1926.

G22 Oslo County   Statistical Yearbook 1939. Oslo, 1940.

Publications of the United Nations

G23 United Nations

Sex and Age of International Migrants: 1918-1947.
Pop. Studies No. 11. Dep. of Social Affairs,
Pop. Div., New York, 1953.

G24 United Nations

The Determinants and Consequences of Population
Trends. Pop. Studies No. 17. Dep. of Social
Affairs, Pop. Div., New York, 1953.

Official Statistics of the United States

G25 Abramovitz, M.

Statement in: Hearings before the Joint Economic
Committee, 86th Cong., 1st Sess., Pt. 2, Historical and Comparative Rates of Production, Productivity, and Prices.
Washington, 1959, pp. 411-466.

G26 U.S. Census 1890

Compendium. Part II. Washington, D.C., 1892.

G27 U.S. Census 1910

Vol. I. Population. Washington, D.C., 1912.

G28 U.S. Immigration Commission

Occupations of the First and Second
Generations of Immigrants in the United
States. Senate Document No. 282.
Washington, D.C., 1911.

G29 U.S. Immigration Commission

Abstracts of Reports of the Immigration
Commission. Vol. I. Senate Document
No. 747, Washington, D.C., 1911.

DISSERTATIONS IN EUROPEAN ECONOMIC HISTORY

An Arno Press Collection

Atkin, John Michael. **British Overseas Investment, 1918-1931** (Doctoral Dissertation, University of London, 1968). 1977

Brosselin, Arlette. **Les Forêts De La Côte D'Or Au XIXème Siècle, et L'Utilisation De Leurs Produits** (Doctoral Thesis, Université de Dijon, 1973). 1977

Brumont, Francis. **La Bureba A L'Époque De Philippe II** (Doctoral Dissertation, Université de Toulouse, 1974). 1977

Cohen, Jon S. **Finance and Industrialization in Italy, 1894-1914** (Doctoral Dissertation, University of California, Berkeley, 1966). 1977

Dagneau, Jacques. **Les Agences Régionales Du Crédit Lyonnais, Années 1870-1914** (Doctoral Thesis, Université de Paris-VIII, 1975). 1977

Dennis, Kenneth G. **'Competition' in the History of Economic Thought** (Doctoral Dissertation, Oxford University, 1975). 1977

Desert, Gabriel. **Une Société Rurale Au XIXe Siècle:** Les Paysans Du Calvados, 1815-1895 (Doctoral Dissertation, Université de Paris, Sorbonne, 1971). 1977

Fierain, Jacques. **Les Raffineries De Sucre Des Ports En France:** XIXe -- début du XXe siècles (Doctoral Dissertation, Université de Nantes, 1974). 1977

Goreux, Louis-Marie. **Agricultural Productivity and Economic Development in France, 1852-1950** (Doctoral Dissertation, University of Chicago, 1955). With the Revised French Version. 1977

Guignet, Philippe. **Mines, Manufactures et Ouvriers Du Valenciennois Au XVIIIe Siècle** (Doctoral Dissertation, Université de Lille III, 1976). Two vols. in one. 1977

Haines, Michael R. **Economic-Demographic Interrelations in Developing Agricultural Regions:** A Case Study of Prussian Upper Silesia, 1840-1914 (Doctoral Dissertation, University of Pennsylvania, 1971). 1977

Hohorst, Gerd. **Wirtschaftswachstum Und Bevölkerungsentwicklung In Preussen 1816 Bis 1914** (Doctoral Dissertation, University of Münster, 1977). 1977

Huertas, Thomas Francis. **Economic Growth and Economic Policy in a Multinational Setting:** The Habsburg Monarchy, 1841-1865 (Doctoral Dissertation, University of Chicago, 1977). 1977

Jankowski, Manfred. **Public Policy in Industrial Growth:** The Case of the Early Ruhr Mining Region, 1766-1865 (Doctoral Dissertation, University of Wisconsin, 1969). 1977

Jefferys, James B. **Business Organisation in Great Britain, 1856-1914** (Doctoral Dissertation, University of London, 1938). 1977

Kirchhain, Günter. **Das Wachstum Der Deutschen Baumwollindustrie Im 19. Jahrhundert** (Doctoral Dissertation, University of Münster, 1973). 1977

Von Laer, Hermann. **Industrialisierung Und Qualität Der Arbeit Eine Bildungsökonomische Untersuchung Für Das 19. Jahrhundert** (Doctoral Dissertation, University of Münster, 1975). 1977

Lee, W. R. **Population Growth, Economic Development and Social Change in Bavaria, 1750-1850** (Revised Doctoral Dissertation, University of Oxford, 1972). 1977

LeVeen, E. Phillip. **British Slave Trade Suppression Policies, 1821-1865** (Doctoral Dissertation, University of Chicago, 1972). 1977

Metzer, Jacob. **Some Economic Aspects of Railroad Development in Tsarist Russia** (Doctoral Dissertation, University of Chicago, 1972). 1977

Moe, Thorvald. **Demographic Developments and Economic Growth in Norway, 1740-1940** (Doctoral Dissertation, Stanford University, 1970). 1977

Mueller, Reinhold C. **The Procuratori di San Marco and the Venetian Credit Market:** A Study of the Development of Credit and Banking in the Trecento (Doctoral Dissertation, Johns Hopkins University, 1969). 1977

Neuburger, Hugh. **German Banks and German Economic Growth from Unification to World War I** (Doctoral Dissertation, University of Chicago, 1974). 1977

Newell, William Henry. **Population Change and Agricultural Developments in Nineteenth Century France** (Doctoral Dissertation, University of Pennsylvania, 1971). 1977

Saly, Pierre. **La Politique Des Grands Travaux En France, 1929-1939** (Doctoral Dissertation, Université de Paris VIII, Vincennes, 1975). 1977

Shrimpton, Colin. **The Landed Society and the Farming Community of Essex in the Late Eighteenth and Early Nineteenth Centuries** (Doctoral Dissertation, Cambridge University, 1965). 1977

Tortella[-Casares], Gabriel. **Banking, Railroads, and Industry in Spain, 1829-1874** (Doctoral Dissertation, University of Wisconsin, 1972). 1977

Viallon, Jean-Baptiste. **La Croissance Agricole En France Et En Bourgogne De 1850 A Nos Jours** (Doctoral Dissertation, Université de Dijon, 1976). 1977

Villiers, Patrick. **Le Commerce Colonial Atlantique Et La Guerre D'Indépendance Des États Unis D'Amérique, 1778-1783** (Doctoral Dissertation, Université de Paris I, Pantheon-Sorbonne, 1975). 1977

Walters, R. H. **The Economic and Business History of the South Wales Steam Coal Industry, 1840-1914** (Doctoral Dissertation, Oxford University, 1975). 1977